Language Arts
Grade 5

ISBN 978-0-544-26788-6

1 2 3 4 5 6 7 8 9 10   0982   22 21 20 19 18 17 16 15 14

4500460777   A B C D E F G

Core Skills Language Arts
GRADE 5
Table of Contents

Unit 3: Mechanics

Unit 4: Vocabulary and Usage

Unit 5: Writing

Unit 6: Research Skills

*Aligns to the English Language Arts Common Core State Standards for grade 5.

Table of Contents
Core Skills Language Arts, Grade 5

Introduction

Core Skills Language Arts was developed to help students improve the language skills they need to succeed. The book emphasizes skills in the key areas of

- grammar
- punctuation
- vocabulary
- writing
- research

The more than 100 lessons included in the book provide many opportunities for students to practice and apply important language and writing skills. These skills will help students excel in all academic areas, increase their scores on standardized tests, and have a greater opportunity for success in their careers.

About the Book

The book is divided into six units:

- Parts of Speech
- Sentences
- Mechanics
- Vocabulary and Usage
- Writing
- Research Skills

Students can work through each unit of the book, or focus on specific areas for extra practice.

Lessons have specific instructions and examples and are designed for students to complete independently. Grammar lessons range from using nouns and verbs to constructing better sentences. Writing exercises range from the opinion paragraph to the research report. With this practice, students will gain extra confidence as they work on daily school lessons or standardized tests.

A thorough answer key is also provided to check the quality of answers.

A Step Toward Success

Practice may not always make perfect, but it is certainly a step in the right direction. The activities in *Core Skills Language Arts* are an excellent way to ensure greater success for students.

Nouns

> A **noun** is a word that names a person, a place, a thing, or an idea.
>
> Use exact nouns to make clear pictures.
>
> *Examples:*   person = girl   place = park   thing = door   idea = freedom

**Read each sentence. Write the nouns. Write *person, place, thing,*
or *idea* after each noun to tell what the noun names.**

1. Our sense of smell is located in the nose.

_____

2. Most people like the smell of delicious food, mowed grass, and clean rain.

_____

3. People get much enjoyment from these special odors.

_____

4. Rotten eggs produce an unpleasant odor.

_____

5. The sense of smell can protect a person from danger.

_____

Rewrite each sentence. Replace the underlined nouns with more exact words.

6. José likes the smells of <u>meat</u> cooking and <u>dessert</u> baking.

_____

_____

7. José and Frank sat in the <u>room</u> waiting for their <u>meal</u>.

_____

_____

Common Nouns and Proper Nouns

A **common noun** names any person, place, or thing. It begins with a lowercase letter.

Examples: writer   state   month

A **proper noun** names a particular person, place, or thing. Each important word of a proper noun begins with a capital letter.

Examples: Fred Gipson   Hawaii   February

Read the sentences. Underline each common noun and circle each proper noun. Rewrite each sentence, replacing the common and proper nouns with different ones.

1. The young scientist was born in Maryland.

   _____

2. Many friends helped Benjamin Banneker.

   _____

3. People throughout the United States still recall his accomplishments.

   _____

   _____

4. Banneker helped design Washington, D.C.

   _____

5. This man had an unusually good memory.

   _____

6. The astronomer spent many nights watching the stars and planets.

   _____

7. Now, scientists are exploring Mars, Jupiter, and other planets.

   _____

   _____

8. What would Banneker think of the changes in his country?

   _____

Singular and Plural Nouns

> A **singular noun** names one person, place, thing, or idea.
>
> *Examples:* hog   blouse   fox   liberty
>
> A **plural noun** names more than one person, place, thing, or idea.
> Make most nouns plural by adding *s* or *es*.
>
> *Examples:* hogs   blouses   foxes   liberties

Write each underlined noun. Then, write *singular* or *plural* to tell what kind of noun it is.

1. A <u>tornado</u> does not last as long as a <u>hurricane</u> does.

   _____

2. A tornado usually lasts only <u>minutes</u>, or at the most a few <u>hours</u>.

   _____

3. Its <u>winds</u> are much stronger than a hurricane's.

   _____

4. The hot <u>air</u> from a large forest <u>fire</u> can cause a tornado.

   _____

5. Certain weather <u>conditions</u> are warning <u>signs</u> for a tornado.

   _____

Rewrite each sentence. Change each underlined singular noun to a plural noun. Make any other changes that are necessary.

6. The <u>girl</u> ate her <u>lunch</u> on the school <u>bench</u>.

   _____

7. The young <u>lady</u> looked at the dark <u>cloud</u> overhead.

   _____

8. A strong <u>wind</u> picked up a <u>box</u> of books by the library <u>door</u>.

   _____

   _____

Special Plural Nouns

Some nouns change spelling in the plural form. Other nouns have the same singular and plural form.

Examples:

Change Spelling	**Same Singular and Plural**
woman—women	salmon
child—children	elk
tooth—teeth	deer
goose—geese	trout
hoof—hooves	sheep

Complete each sentence by writing the plural form of the noun in ( ).

1. Lisa caught four special _____ in that stream.
(trout)

2. These _____ told Lisa a story.
(fish)

3. They said that they were really _____.
(hero)

4. Two of them were really _____.
(woman)

5. The other two were really _____.
(man)

6. They had chased out all the _____ from their village.
(mouse)

7. This went against the _____ of the other people in the village.
(belief)

8. The village people thought mice protected them from _____.
(wolf)

9. For a while, there had been four _____ in a field.
(ox)

10. Then, they had been turned into _____ in a barnyard.
(calf)

11. All the _____ in the village made fun of them.
(child)

12. Finally, their _____ were turned into fins.
(foot)

13. If they could eat bread, their _____ would return to normal.
(life)

Singular Possessive Nouns

A **singular possessive noun** shows ownership by one person or thing.

Add an apostrophe (') and *s* to most singular nouns to show possession.

Examples: Natoh's cat   the cat's whiskers

Write each sentence. Change the underlined words to form a singular possessive noun.

1. The mother <u>of my friend</u> had a baby yesterday.

   _____

2. The teeth <u>of the baby</u> are not in yet.

   _____

3. The head <u>of the child</u> is still soft.

   _____

4. The tie <u>of the bib</u> is torn.

   _____

5. The sheets <u>of the crib</u> are pink.

   _____

6. The smile <u>of the uncle</u> is happy.

   _____

7. The gift <u>of the grandmother</u> is a new blanket.

   _____

8. The pleasure <u>of the father</u> is easy to see.

   _____

9. The eyes <u>of the infant</u> are blue.

   _____

10. The life <u>of my friend</u> will be different now.

    _____

5

Plural Possessive Nouns

A **plural possessive noun** shows ownership by more than one person or thing.

To form the possessive of a plural noun ending in *s* or *es*, add only an apostrophe (').

To form the possessive of a plural noun that does not end in *s*, add an apostrophe and *s* ('*s*).

Examples: trucks' tires   foxes' lair   children's lunches

Write each sentence. Change the underlined words to form a plural possessive noun.

1. Imagine the surprise <u>of the children</u>!

_____

2. They found the baby <u>of the robins</u> on the sidewalk.

_____

3. They returned it to the nest <u>of the parents</u>.

_____

4. They watched the activities <u>of the adult birds</u> for a while.

_____

5. The fear <u>of the animals</u> was apparent.

_____

6. The odor <u>of the humans</u> was on the baby bird.

_____

7. The bird was now the responsibility <u>of the young people</u>.

_____

8. The job <u>of the students</u> was to find a shoe box.

_____

9. The job <u>of the parents</u> was to find some soft lining.

_____

Pronouns

A **pronoun** is a word that takes the place of one or more nouns.

Use pronouns to avoid repeating words.

A **singular pronoun** replaces a singular noun. The words *I, me, you, he, she, him, her,* and *it* are singular pronouns. Always capitalize the pronoun *I.*

A **plural pronoun** replaces a plural noun. The words *we, you, they, us,* and *them* are plural pronouns.

Examples: The woman thought *she* should go to the store.
(*She* takes the place of *the woman.*)
The travelers searched for a place *they* could spend the night.
(*They* takes the place of *the travelers.*)

Read each pair of sentences. Draw a line under the pronoun in the second sentence. Circle the word or words in the first sentence that the pronoun replaces.

1. Explorers came to Australia.
   They were amazed by the strange native animals and plants.

2. An animal the size of a greyhound lived there.
   It could leap like a grasshopper.

3. These animals are now known as kangaroos.
   Some of them can cover 27 feet in one jump.

4. Two interesting birds of Australia are emus and cassowaries.
   They cannot fly.

5. The early explorers told about the platypus.
   It is a mammal that lays eggs.

6. Scientists of the time did not believe the stories.
   They thought the stories were lies.

7. The coolabah of Western Australia is an interesting tree.
   It can survive frost as well as 120-degree heat.

8. The official flower of Western Australia is called the kangaroo paw.
   It looks like a paw and is even furry to the touch.

9. The grass trees are distantly related to lilies.
   They grow grassy leaves and put up spikes with white flowers.

10. The trunks of the bottle trees are very interesting.
    Like bottles, they come in many sizes, sometimes six feet around.

Subject Pronouns

A **subject pronoun** takes the place of one or more nouns in the subject of a sentence. The words *I, you, he, she, it, we,* and *they* are subject pronouns.

Examples: *He* brought a rat to school.
                 We do not like rats.
                 You can pet the rat.

Rewrite each sentence. Replace the underlined word or words with a subject pronoun.

1. <u>My brother and I</u> read about the Wrights last week.

_____

2. It was <u>my brother</u> who found the book.

_____

3. <u>Wilbur and Orville Wright</u> grew up in Dayton, Ohio.

_____

4. <u>Their father</u> was a bishop there.

_____

5. <u>Their older sister, Katharine,</u> helped care for them.

_____

6. <u>A toy bicycle</u> was a gift from their father.

_____

7. <u>Wilbur Wright</u> was four years older than Orville.

_____

8. On December 17, 1903, <u>the world's first airplane flight</u> took place.

_____

9. <u>The first flight</u> lasted 12 seconds.

_____

10. <u>The next three flights</u> were 13 seconds, 15 seconds, and 59 seconds.

_____

Object Pronouns

An **object pronoun** follows an action verb, such as *see* or *tell,* or a word such as *about, at, for, from, near, of, to,* or *with.*

The words *me, you, him, her, it, us,* and *them* are object pronouns.

Examples: Chen took *it* to school.
Grandpa had a gift for *me.*
My cousin saw *you.*

Rewrite each sentence. Replace the underlined word or words with an object pronoun.

1. Darkness covered the pine woods, the swamp, and the game wardens.

_____

2. The game wardens noticed the light.

_____

3. Then, the game wardens saw the alligator poachers.

_____

4. Two men and a woman were searching the lake for alligators.

_____

5. The game wardens pushed their boat out of the brush.

_____

6. They raced toward the poachers.

_____

7. The powerful engine moved the boat quickly over the water.

_____

8. The poachers quickly dumped two alligators back into the water.

_____

9. The wardens searched the inside of the poachers' boat.

_____

Subject or Object Pronoun?

> Remember that pronouns can be subjects or objects in sentences.

Choose the pronoun in ( ) that correctly completes each sentence. Write it on the line. Then, circle *subject pronoun* **or** *object pronoun.*

1. _____ has studied kung fu for years.
   (He, Him)

   subject pronoun   *object pronoun*

2. The history of the martial arts is interesting to _____.
   (he, him)

   subject pronoun   *object pronoun*

3. _____ know about many great warriors.
   (We, Us)

   subject pronoun   *object pronoun*

4. One of _____ was a 13-year-old girl named Shuen Guan.
   (they, them)

   subject pronoun   *object pronoun*

5. _____ lived during the Jinn Dynasty, over 1600 years ago.
   (She, Her)

   subject pronoun   *object pronoun*

6. Her people had a nickname for _____.
   (she, her)

   subject pronoun   *object pronoun*

7. _____ called her "Little Tigress."
   (They, Them)

   subject pronoun   *object pronoun*

8. When her town was attacked by bandits, no one would fight _____.
   (they, them)

   subject pronoun   *object pronoun*

9. _____ was the only one brave enough.
   (She, Her)

   subject pronoun   *object pronoun*

10. Shuen Guan fought her way through _____ and went for help.
    (they, them)

    subject pronoun   *object pronoun*

Reflexive Pronouns

A **reflexive pronoun** refers to the subject of a sentence. The words *myself, yourself, himself, herself,* and *itself* are singular reflexive pronouns. *Ourselves, yourselves,* and *themselves* are plural reflexive pronouns.

Choose the reflexive pronoun in ( ) that correctly completes each sentence. Write the pronoun on the line.

1. I will help _____ enjoy this vacation.
   (myself, ourselves)

2. Last year Jerry bought _____ a book about Australia.
   (himself, yourself)

3. The book concerned _____ with the history of the land.
   (itself, themselves)

4. Jerry's sister Joan made _____ read the book.
   (herself, ourselves)

5. "Jerry and Joan, teach _____ about Australia before our vacation," their mother said.
   (yourself, yourselves)

6. "That way, we can all enjoy _____ more," she continued.
   (myself, ourselves)

7. "Joan, buy _____ a good pair of walking shoes before the trip," said her father.
   (yourself, yourselves)

Write a reflexive pronoun on each line to complete the sentence.

8. My sister and I will be treating _____ to a trip.

9. She still has to buy _____ a ticket.

10. I have bought _____ some new clothes for the trip.

11. Susan, our travel agent, taught _____ the travel business.

12. Her partner, Mark, talked _____ into learning it, too.

Possessive Pronouns

A **possessive pronoun** shows ownership. Some possessive pronouns come before a noun. Some stand alone. Some possessive pronouns are *my, your, his, her, its, our,* and *their.*

Examples: Joe lost *his* glove.
He lost it in *your* barn.
The new car is *ours.*

Underline the possessive pronoun in each sentence. Then, write *before a noun* or *stands alone* to tell the kind of possessive pronoun used.

1. The members of the Dallas club wanted to send their team to the Olympic trials.

   _____

2. Its membership included just one person. _____

3. Babe Didrikson was proud that the position would be hers. _____

4. Her teammates were proud of Didrikson, too. _____

5. They knew that, at the end of the trials, the championship would be theirs.

   _____

6. "All our fans will be supporting you," they told Didrikson. _____

Write the pronoun in ( ) that correctly completes each sentence.

7. Didrikson's fans were always impressed by the range of _____ athletic abilities.
   (her, hers)

8. Two gold medals were _____ at the end of the 1932 Olympic Games.
   (her, hers)

9. Many fans followed her varied career, and she appreciated all _____ attention.
   (their, theirs)

10. Of all the sports in which she competed, _____ favorite is swimming.
    (your, yours)

Agreement of Pronouns

A pronoun is a word that takes the place of one or more nouns. Pronouns show number and gender. Number tells whether a pronoun is singular or plural. Gender tells whether the pronoun is masculine, feminine, or neuter.

The **antecedent** of a pronoun is the noun or nouns to which the pronoun refers. A pronoun should agree with its antecedent in number and gender.

Write the pronoun that correctly completes the second sentence in each pair. Then, circle the pronoun's antecedent in the first sentence.

1. Mr. Les Harsten did an experiment with plants. _____ investigated with sound.

2. The man used two banana plants. He exposed _____ to the same amount of light.

3. Les also gave both plants the same amount of warmth and water. _____ did, however, change one thing.

4. One of the plants was exposed to a special sound for an hour a day. _____ was a high-pitched hum.

5. That plant grew faster. In fact, _____ was 70 percent taller than the other plant.

6. All sounds won't work this way. Some of _____ can harm plants.

7. A recording of Harsten's sound is being sold. _____ is used by some plant growers.

8. Classical music works just as well with plants. _____ seem to thrive on it.

9. Hard rock music, however, does not work. _____ can stunt their growth.

10. You may want to play music for your plants. _____ may like it.

Adjectives

An **adjective** is a word that describes a noun or pronoun.
Adjectives can tell how many, what color, or what size or shape.
They can also describe how something feels, sounds, tastes, or smells.

You usually separate two adjectives with a comma.

Use vivid adjectives to paint clear word pictures.

Examples: *Two* eggs were in the nest.
                 The *blue* stone was in a *small* box.
                 The *fat* cat has *soft* fur.

**Write each adjective that describes the underlined nouns. Then, write *what kind* or *how many*
to identify what the adjective tells about the noun.**

1. The azalea is a spectacular <u>plant</u>.

   _____

2. It has superb, beautiful <u>flowers</u>.

   _____

3. It will grow wherever winter <u>temperatures</u> are not too low.

   _____

4. There are about twelve different <u>types</u> of azaleas.

   _____

5. You can find azaleas with red, pink, violet, or white <u>flowers</u>.

   _____

6. Azaleas do best in spongy, acid <u>soil</u>.

   _____

7. They should be fed three or four <u>times</u> between the end of the flowering <u>season</u> and September.

   _____

8. Sweet, fragrant <u>flowers</u> make the camellia a special <u>plant</u>.

   _____

Proper Adjectives

> A **proper adjective** is formed from a proper noun.
>
> Capitalize each important word in a proper adjective.

Underline the proper adjective in each sentence. On the line, write the proper noun from which it is formed. Use a dictionary if you need help.

1. Our modern Olympics come from an ancient Greek tradition.

   _____

2. The chariot races were often won by Spartan men.

   _____

3. An Athenian racer won three times in a row, starting in 536 B.C.

   _____

4. After 146 B.C., Roman athletes also competed in the games.

   _____

5. The 1988 Olympics took place in the Korean city of Seoul.

   _____

6. In 1976, a young Romanian girl, Nadia Comaneci, had seven perfect scores in gymnastics.

   _____

Complete each sentence by writing a proper adjective on the line. Form the proper adjective from the proper noun in ( ).

7. Gertrude Ederle was the first woman to swim the _____ Channel.
   (England)

8. Sonja Henie was a famous _____ ice-skater.
   (Norway)

9. Barbara Ann Scott was a _____ ice-skater.
   (Canada)

10. Several _____ skaters have won awards in international competition.
    (America)

Predicate Adjectives

An adjective is a word that describes a noun. A **predicate adjective** follows a linking verb such as *is, seems,* or *looks.* When an adjective follows a linking verb, it can describe the subject of the sentence.

In some sentences, different adjectives in different positions describe the same noun or pronoun.

Examples: Sam is *young* and *bold.*
That snake looks *scary.*

Circle the adjective or adjectives following the linking verb in each sentence. Write the noun or pronoun the adjective describes.

1. These peanuts are crunchy. _____

2. They taste very salty. _____

3. The skin on the peanut is red. _____

4. Those pumpkin seeds look delicious. _____

5. Pumpkin seeds once seemed inedible. _____

6. They have grown popular lately. _____

7. Some quick snacks are healthful. _____

8. Green apples are sometimes sour. _____

9. This common fruit is crisp and juicy. _____

10. A crisp vegetable can be noisy if you eat it. _____

Write two adjectives to complete each sentence.

11. Bananas are _____.

12. Pickles taste _____.

13. Candy canes usually look _____.

14. During the summer, watermelons become _____.

15. With enough rain, pole beans will grow _____.

Unit 1
Core Skills Language Arts, Grade 5

Articles and Demonstrative Adjectives

The adjectives *a, an,* and *the* are called **articles**. Use *a* before a word that begins with a consonant sound. Use *an* before a word that begins with a vowel sound. Use *the* before a word that begins with a consonant or a vowel.

This, that, these, and *those* are called **demonstrative adjectives**.

Examples: Have you ever seen *an* owl?
The owl is *a* nocturnal animal.
That owl scared *those* people.

Choose the adjective in ( ) that best completes each sentence. Write it on the line.

1. Many people have _____ strange idea about naturalists.
   (a, an)

2. _____ people regard naturalists as weird.
   (This, These)

3. They think naturalists wander around in forests, eating roots and berries along

   _____ way.
   (an, the)

4. Not all naturalists fit _____ description.
   (this, those)

5. You could be _____ naturalist yourself.
   (a, an)

6. You could learn _____ names of trees.
   (a, the)

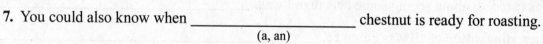

7. You could also know when _____ chestnut is ready for roasting.
   (a, an)

8. You could tell whether _____ clay is better than that clay.
   (this, these)

9. You could learn all _____ things easily.
   (this, these)

10. You could become one of _____ weird naturalists, too!
    (that, those)

Adjectives That Compare

> Add *er* to most short adjectives to compare two nouns or pronouns. Add *est* to most short adjectives to compare more than two nouns or pronouns. Change the *y* to *i* before adding *er* or *est* to adjectives that end in a consonant and *y*.
>
> Use *more* with some adjectives to compare two nouns or pronouns. Use *most* with some adjectives to compare more than two nouns or pronouns.
>
> *Examples:*   This building is *taller* than that one.
> The whale is the *largest* of all animals.
> Diving is *more interesting* to watch than golf.
> It may be the *most difficult* of all sports.

Write the correct form of the adjective in ( ) to complete each sentence.

1. Our trip to New Mexico was even (wonderful) than I expected. _____

2. The mountains there are the (beautiful) I have ever seen. _____

3. We saw Wheeler Peak, the (high) point in the state. _____

4. We visited a mine shaft that was (deep) than a mile. _____

5. Mining is one of the (big) industries in New Mexico. _____

6. Albuquerque is the (large) city in New Mexico. _____

7. It is also the (easy) city to reach by plane. _____

8. The (unusual) place we saw was Carlsbad Caverns. _____

9. We had never seen (strange) rocks than those. _____

10. My brother was (excited) about seeing some bats than I was. _____

11. To me, the (interesting) place of all was Santa Fe. _____

12. It is one of the (old) cities in North America. _____

Special Forms of Adjectives That Compare

Some adjectives have special forms for comparing.

Examples: Trixi has a *good* story.
                Chad's story is *better* than Trixi's.
                Teena's story is the *best* of all.

Adjective	Comparing Two Things	Comparing More Than Two Things
good	better	best
bad	worse	worst
little	less	least
much	more	most
many	more	most

Complete each sentence by choosing the correct form of the adjective in ( ). Write it on the line.

1. Hunger brought the Irish to America for a _____ life.
   (better, best)

2. About half of Ireland's farms had _____ than three acres of land.
   (less, least)

3. They had had the _____ potato crop in years.
   (worse, worst)

4. Each day _____ people were starving than the day before.
   (many, more)

5. Queen Victoria was told that the situation was becoming _____ every day.
   (worse, worst)

6. She visited Ireland and said that she saw _____ ragged and wretched people than
   she had seen anywhere else.
   (more, most)

7. _____ Irish people chose Boston as their new home.
   (Many, Much)

8. Boston was the _____ convenient city for them because many ships stopped
   there first.
   (more, most)

9. Each immigrant hoped that life in the new country would be _____ than in the
   old country.
   (good, better)

10. Most Irish immigrants thought America to be the _____ place in the world to live.
    (better, best)

Action Verbs and Linking Verbs

A **verb** expresses action or being.

An **action verb** is a word or group of words that expresses an action. An action verb is often the key word in the predicate. It tells what the subject does.

A **linking verb** connects the subject of a sentence with a word or words in the predicate. The most common linking verb is *be*. Some forms of *be* are *am, is, are, was,* and *were*. Here are other common linking verbs: *become, feel, seem, look, grow, taste, appear,* and *smell*.

Examples: King Uther *ruled* England a long time ago. (action)
The name of his baby boy *was* Arthur. (linking)
In time, Sir Ector *became* Arthur's guardian. (linking)

Read each sentence. Underline each action verb. Circle each linking verb.

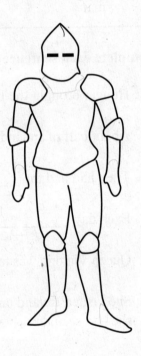

1. Young Arthur felt very nervous.

2. Sir Kay left his sword at the inn.

3. He needed his sword for the tournament that day.

4. Arthur looked all over the village for a replacement.

5. Suddenly, Arthur saw a sword in a stone.

6. He ran over to the stone and studied the strange sword.

7. It appeared very secure in its stony sheath.

8. Arthur pulled it, and it moved.

9. The sword slid from the stone easily!

10. Arthur hurried back to the tournament with his prize.

11. Sir Ector bowed deeply to his foster son.

12. The sword was the sign of the next king of England.

Main Verbs and Helping Verbs

> Sometimes a simple predicate is made up of two or more verbs. The **main verb** is the most important verb in the predicate. It comes last in a group of verbs.
>
> A **helping verb** can work with the main verb to tell about an action. The helping verb always comes before the main verb. These words are often used as helping verbs: *am, is, are, was, were, has, have, had,* and *will.*
>
> Sometimes another word comes between a main verb and a helping verb.

Choose the correct form of the verb in ( ) to complete each sentence. Write the word in the sentence. Then, write *main verb* or *helping verb*.

1. Inez has _____ Greek legends to children for many years.

   (tell, told, telling) _____

2. The children were _____ forward to the next story.

   (look, looked, looking) _____

3. "I shall _____ the children the legend of Narcissus," she thought.

   (tell, told, telling) _____

4. Narcissus _____ hunting one day.

   (shall, have, was) _____

5. He had _____ over a mountain pool for a drink.

   (lean, leaned, leaning) _____

6. He _____ gazing at his own reflection in the water.

   (are, was, were) _____

7. Narcissus had _____ in love with his own face.

   (fall, fallen, falling) _____

8. The next moment, a flower _____ growing where Narcissus had stood.

   (am, are, was) _____

Name _____ Date _____

Present-Tense Verbs

A **present-tense verb** tells about actions that are happening now.

Add *s* or *es* to most present-tense verbs when the subject of the sentence is *he, she, it,* or a singular noun.

Do not add *s* or *es* to a present-tense verb when the subject is *I, you, we, they,* or a plural noun.

Examples: Dougal Dixon *writes* books that stretch the reader's imagination.
His ideas *mix* science and fiction in an exciting way.
The neck of the lank *reaches* high into the air like a giraffe's.
The harridan *flies* with wings that fold up when it *walks.*

Write the present-tense form of the verb in ( ) that correctly completes each sentence.

1. Cathy _____ the flower shop down the street.
   (like)

2. She _____ it about once a week.
   (visit)

3. She _____ home with armfuls of flowers.
   (come)

4. Her sisters _____ attractive arrangements.
   (fix)

5. Sometimes Cathy _____ carnations, roses, and irises in her vases.
   (mix)

6. Her sister Gladys _____ pictures of the flowers.
   (take)

7. They _____ the pictures to the owners of the shop.
   (show)

8. Cathy _____ for a job at the shop.
   (wish)

9. The owner of the shop _____ about the business.
   (worry)

10. She _____ her costs very closely.
    (watch)

11. The shop _____ a good profit.
    (make)

12. Maybe the owner _____ to hire Cathy.
    (need)

Past-Tense Verbs

A **past-tense verb** tells about actions that happened in the past.

Add *ed* or *d* to most present-tense verbs to make them show past tense. You may have to drop an *e,* double a final consonant, or change a *y* to an *i.*

Examples: When Mr. King was a boy, he *lived* on a farm.
He always *carried* his lunch to school.
He *dipped* water from a nearby spring.

Write the past-tense form of each verb in ( ) to complete each sentence.

1. We _____ to the food fair.
(walk)

2. I _____ many different foods.
(sample)

3. Indian curry _____ both spicy and sweet.
(seem)

4. Colorful signs _____ the unusual treats.
(describe)

5. A Greek restaurant _____ baklava made from
(serve)

   nuts, honey, and flaky pastry.

6. My friend _____ a glass of African root beer.
(sip)

7. A woman _____ spring rolls made of shrimp and vegetables.
(fry)

8. I _____ many tasty foods that day.
(try)

9. One chef _____ me a red carnation.
(pass)

10. I _____ the flower to my shirt.
(pin)

11. All of the meals _____ fresh vegetables and fruit.
(feature)

12. We _____ many unusual ones.
(taste)

Future-Tense Verbs

A **future-tense verb** expresses action that will happen in the future.

To form the future tense of a verb, use the helping verb *will* with the main verb.

Examples: Sam *will live* in the woods all year.
He *will learn* about many things.

Sometimes other words appear between the helping verb and the main verb.

Examples: Sam *will* not *go* back to his home.
Will he *have* a hard time in the winter?

Complete each sentence. Write the future tense of the verb in ( ).

1. What _____ _____ to Sam in the next few months?
(happen)

2. He _____ _____ for game.
(hunt)

3. He _____ _____ food at harvest time.
(gather)

4. _____ Sam _____ his family?
(miss)

5. _____ they _____ for him in the woods?
(search)

6. They probably _____ not _____ him.
(find)

7. Sam _____ - _____ David, his friend.
(remember)

8. Perhaps Sam _____ _____ something different.
(cook)

9. Maybe Sam _____ _____ down the river on his new raft.
(float)

10. No matter what, Sam _____ _____.
(hide)

11. No one _____ _____ him.
(notice)

12. _____ Sam _____ the woods?
(leave)

Which Tense Is It?

Remember that a present-tense verb tells about actions that are happening now. A past-tense verb tells about actions that happened in the past. A future-tense verb shows action that will happen in the future.

Underline the verb in each sentence. Then write *present, past,* or *future* to identify the tense.

1. Lizards look different from snakes. _____

2. For one thing, they have legs. _____

3. A gecko lizard climbs across a ceiling. _____

4. Suction cups on its feet make this possible. _____

5. That lizard climbed the hill. _____

6. That other lizard jumped very high. _____

7. Samuel will see many lizards at the zoo. _____

8. He will go to the zoo on Tuesday. _____

9. We will ride to the zoo on a bus. _____

10. The zoo guide will tell us all about lizards. _____

Change each present-tense verb to the correct future-tense form. Rewrite the sentence on the line.

11. Sam sees ten lizards.

_____

12. I see only four.

_____

13. Some lizards change colors.

_____

Perfect Tenses

The **perfect tense** indicates action that has already been completed or will be completed. Perfect tense can be used in the present, past, or future tense.

Putting words such as *today, yesterday,* or *tomorrow* in front of a statement helps you know whether the tense should be present, past, or future perfect.

Examples:	**Present Perfect (today)**	**Past Perfect (yesterday)**	**Future Perfect (tomorrow)**
	I have seen.	I had seen.	I will have seen.
	You have greeted me.	You had greeted me.	You will have greeted me.
	He has walked.	He had walked.	He will have walked.
	She has sung.	She had sung.	She will have sung.
	We have finished.	We had finished.	We will have finished.
	They have left home.	They had left home.	They will have left home.

Fill in the blank with the correct perfect-tense form of the verb in ( ).

1. Yesterday Tony _____ an hour fixing his bike's flat tire.
   (spend)

2. Today he _____ that the tire is slowly deflating again.
   (find)

3. By tomorrow afternoon he _____ it to a shop for professional help.
   (take)

4. Last week I _____ out a new book from the library.
   (check)

5. This week I _____ 50 pages of my book.
   (read)

6. Next week I _____ the book so I can return it.
   (finish)

7. Joe told me last Tuesday that he _____ a new fitness plan.
   (start)

8. So far this week Joe _____ four miles.
   (walk)

9. By the end of the month, Joe _____ twenty miles.
   (go)

10. Jillian _____ about her math exam all month.
    (worry)

11. She told me, "I _____ more for this test than for any other!"
    (study)

Consistent Tense

Keeping your verb tenses **consistent**, or the same, helps your reader understand the action. Carelessly mixing present, past, and future tense can make it unclear just what is happening in a story.

Example: Akio *worked* on his art project all morning. Then he *eats* lunch with his dad. Finally, he *will go* for a run. (inconsistent)

Akio *worked* on his art project all morning. Then he *ate* lunch with his dad. Finally, he *went* for a run. (consistent)

Each pair of sentences has an error in verb tense. Circle the incorrect verb and rewrite the sentence.

1. Yesterday Talya writes a sentence on the board. Then she went back to her seat.

_____

2. Patrick is a fast swimmer. He usually beat all the other competitors at a swim meet.

_____

3. The wind often will blow leaves down our street. Then they crunch under my boots.

_____

4. Ms. Martin goes to Norway last year. She studied the culture for many months before her trip.

_____

Each sentence has three verbs. Change two of the verbs to match the third so that the sentence makes sense. Rewrite the sentence.

5. The kitten scampered up the tree, jumps onto a branch, and will look down at the dog.

_____

6. My grandmother reads a cartoon, will think about it, and laughed.

_____

7. Harold will write a letter, stamped the envelope, and waits for a response.

_____

8. Frieda built a tree house, will ride her bike four miles, and eats dinner with her brother.

_____

Irregular Verbs

An **irregular verb** is a verb that does not end with *ed* to show past tense. Some irregular verbs show the perfect tenses by using a different form of the main verb with *have, has,* or *had.*

Examples:	**Present**	**Past**	**Perfect Tenses**
	do, does	did	(have, has, had) done
	come, comes	came	(have, has, had) come
	run, runs	ran	(have, has, had) run
	go, goes	went	(have, has, had) gone

Write the past-tense or perfect-tense form of the verb in ( ) that correctly completes each sentence.

1. Allison has _____ a report on chameleons.
   (do)

2. She _____ a bus to the zoo to do research.
   (ride)

3. She _____ some change to the bus driver.
   (give)

4. At the zoo, Allison _____ from the entrance to the lizard area.
   (run)

5. The chameleons had _____ out into the sunlight.
   (come)

6. She _____ her lunch and watched the lizards.
   (eat)

7. She _____ several chameleons, each a different color.
   (see)

8. The guide had _____ hello to her.
   (say)

9. Allison _____ twelve photos of the reptiles for her report.
   (take)

10. She had _____ about her report for weeks.
    (think)

11. She had _____ a rough draft already.
    (write)

12. That afternoon, she _____ home and worked on the report.
    (go)

More Irregular Verbs

Remember that an irregular verb is a verb that does not end with *ed* to show past tense. Some irregular verbs use *n* or *en* to form the past tense.

Write the past-tense or perfect-tense form of the verb in ( ) that correctly completes each sentence.

1. Wesley _____ a study of Japan last week.
   (begin)

2. One of his mother's friends _____ up in Japan.
   (grow)

3. Wesley has _____ his mother's friend for many years.
   (know)

4. Jinko had _____ to come to America long ago.
   (choose)

5. She had always _____ fondly of her home.
   (speak)

6. Last year Jinko _____ to Japan to visit family and friends.
   (fly)

7. Jinko had _____ a kimono at her wedding.
   (wear)

8. Once, she _____ the pictures of her wedding.
   (lose)

9. She _____ them again last year.
   (find)

10. Her dog had _____ a few of them.
    (tear)

11. One afternoon, Wesley's doorbell _____.
    (ring)

12. Wesley had _____ a cold and had missed school.
    (catch)

13. He had _____ in a pool on a cool evening.
    (swim)

14. Jinko _____ some Japanese music to Wesley's house.
    (bring)

15. She _____ some Japanese songs for Wesley's mother.
    (sing)

Direct Objects

A **direct object** is a noun or pronoun that receives the action of the verb.

Use object pronouns such as *me, you, him, her, it, us,* and *them* as direct objects.

Examples: The country of France gave the *Statue of Liberty* to the United States.
The French government shipped *her* in pieces to the United States.

Read each sentence. Underline the direct object or objects.

1. A team of engineers and laborers constructed her.

2. The Statue of Liberty greeted many immigrants.

3. She carries a torch in her upraised hand.

4. To immigrants, she represents hope and freedom.

5. Ships full of immigrants passed the statue before arriving in America.

Think of a direct object to complete each sentence. Write it in the blank.

6. Millions of immigrants gave up _____ to come to America.

7. Immigrants sought _____ in America.

8. They first visited _____.

9. The immigration agents at Ellis Island questioned the _____.

10. The immigration agents processed _____ slowly.

11. Many immigrants could not speak _____.

12. Starting over in a new country required _____.

13. They faced many _____.

14. Immigrants found _____ in big cities.

15. Big cities also offered _____.

16. Immigrants who spoke the same language established _____.

Adverbs

An **adverb** is a word that describes a verb.

An adverb may tell how, when, or where an action happens. Adverbs that tell how often end in *ly*.

Use adverbs to make your writing vivid. Vary your sentences by moving the adverbs.

Examples: Kristen visited the Science Museum *yesterday*.
She saw an exhibit of holograms *upstairs*.
She *finally* learned why holograms look so real.

Circle the adverb that describes the underlined verb. Then, circle *where, when*, or *how* to indicate what the adverb tells.

1. Daedalus carefully <u>built</u> two pairs of wings.   *where   when   how*

2. First, he <u>collected</u> the feathers of birds.   *where   when   how*

3. Next, he <u>constructed</u> frames of wax.   *where   when   how*

4. Then, he <u>attached</u> the feathers to the frames.   *where   when   how*

5. Finally, he <u>put</u> the wings on himself and on his son, Icarus.   *where   when   how*

6. Daedalus firmly <u>warned</u> Icarus about the sun.   *where   when   how*

7. The warmth of the sun would surely <u>melt</u> the wax.   *where   when   how*

8. The father and son <u>flew</u> joyfully in the sky.   *where   when   how*

9. Icarus <u>flew</u> higher.   *where   when   how*

10. Soon, the sun <u>melted</u> all the wax.   *where   when   how*

11. Icarus <u>fell</u> down into the sea.   *where   when   how*

Add an adverb to make each sentence more vivid. Write the new sentence.

12. Daedalus looked at the surface of the sea.

_____

13. Feathers drifted on the waves.

_____

Adverbs That Compare

Adverbs can be used to compare two or more actions.

When you compare two actions, add *er* to most short adverbs. When you compare more than two actions, add *est* to most short adverbs.

Use *more* and *most* before most adverbs that have two or more syllables. When you compare two actions, use *more*. When you compare more than two, use *most*.

The adverbs *well* and *badly* have special forms of comparison: *well, better, best; badly, worse, worst.*

Examples: Autumn comes *sooner* in Maine than in Virginia.
You must drive *more carefully* in wet weather than in dry weather.
This snowblower works *better* with dry snow than with wet snow.

Write the correct form of the adverb in ( ) to complete each sentence.

1. On August 3, 1492, the sailors aboard three small ships waited _____ than they ever had.
   (eagerly)

2. Their captain had argued _____ than anyone else that the world was round.
   (strongly)

3. Of all the rulers at that time, Queen Isabella of Portugal acted _____.
   (courageously)

4. She believed, _____ than King Ferdinand did, that this was a good idea.
   (completely)

5. Columbus appealed to the queen _____ than another explorer did.
   (often)

6. Of all the explorers at court, Columbus had stated his case _____.
   (convincingly)

Complete each sentence with the correct form of *well* or *badly*.

7. Columbus did _____ than he ever thought possible.
   (well)

8. At times, his crew thought they were doing _____ than any other crew in the history of the world.
   (badly)

9. Columbus had prepared _____ for this trip than for any other trip.
   (well)

10. The three ships were equipped _____ for the journey.
    (well)

Adverbs Before Adjectives and Other Adverbs

> An adverb can be used to describe a verb. An adverb can also be used to describe an adjective or another adverb.
>
> *Example:*   Sheri did a *fairly good* job.
>   She thought *very long* about the question.

Circle the adverb that describes the underlined adjective or adverb.

1. Reiko was sitting very <u>quietly</u> at her desk.

2. She felt extremely <u>interested</u> in the book.

3. The book was about carefully <u>planned</u> Japanese gardens.

4. Reiko quite <u>suddenly</u> decided to make one.

5. She knew her garden couldn't be too <u>big</u>.

6. She had a fairly <u>small</u> yard.

7. It was certainly <u>difficult</u> to choose a type of garden.

8. She considered the rather <u>difficult</u> job of making a garden with a pond.

9. Her yard was much <u>too</u> small for that.

Draw an arrow from the underlined adverb to the adjective, other adverb, or verb it describes.

10. A teahouse garden is <u>particularly</u> charming.

11. It <u>gently</u> suggests an approach to a mountain temple.

12. The builder <u>skillfully</u> uses rocks and stones to suggest mountains and valleys.

13. Reiko didn't think this would work <u>effectively</u> in her yard.

14. She <u>finally</u> decided on a dry landscape garden.

15. A dry landscape garden is <u>much</u> less expensive than a teahouse garden to create.

Adverb or Adjective?

Use an adverb to describe a verb. Use an adjective to describe a noun or pronoun.

Use *good* as an adjective. Use *well* as an adverb or as an adjective to mean "healthy."

Complete each sentence by writing the correct word in ( ).

1. Have you ever brushed up _____ against a stinging nettle?
   (gentle, gently)

2. Were you surprised by the _____ number of stinging sensations?
   (great, greatly)

3. When this happens to you, you might _____ lift up a leaf.
   (careful, carefully)

4. Notice that the underside is _____ covered with sharp bristles.
   (complete, completely)

5. These are _____ attached to sacs of formic acid, the same acid you get from an ant sting.
   (firm, firmly)

6. Nettle stings are not _____.
   (serious, seriously)

7. The pain will go away _____ quickly.
   (fair, fairly)

8. You can dab the _____ area with rubbing alcohol to soothe the pain.
   (entire, entirely)

Complete each sentence with *good* or *well*.

9. Tina and Ted went for a _____ walk in the woods.

10. Tina had not been feeling _____ for a few days.

11. Tina and Ted both walk _____.

12. They had packed a _____ lunch of sandwiches and apples.

Prepositions

A **preposition** is a word that relates a noun or pronoun to other words in the sentence. Some commonly used prepositions are listed below.

above	below	from	through	after	between	into	around
by	of	under	at	during	off	until	before
except	on	up	behind	for	over	without	

The **object of the preposition** is the noun or pronoun that follows the preposition.

Example: I went *to* the store.

A prepositional phrase is a group of words made up of a preposition, its object, and all the words that come between them. Prepositional phrases often tell where, what kind, when, or how.

Example: *At night* she guided her canoe *through the waves*.

Read each sentence. Underline each prepositional phrase. Circle the object of the preposition.

1. The girl returned to her island.

2. A leaking boat had nearly taken her below the waves.

3. She had traveled without any means of navigation except the stars.

4. For many centuries, sailors have found their position by the stars.

5. New developments in the 1700s made navigation easier.

6. However, even modern travelers on the sea use the ancient method of celestial navigation.

7. Navigators take the bearing of a star.

8. A sextant measures a star's angle above the horizon.

9. Sailors can tell their position from that reading.

10. Without this information, navigation would be a hard task.

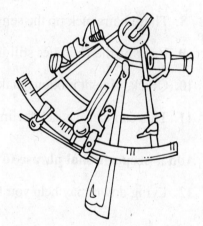

Prepositional Phrases

Remember that a prepositional phrase is made up of a preposition, the object of the preposition, and all the words in between.

Underline each prepositional phrase. Circle the preposition.

1. Did you ever feel seasick in a car?

2. When you are seasick, you are not really sick from the sea.

3. You are sick from the motion of the waves.

4. In this same way, you can get sick in the back of a car.

5. Your sense of balance has been upset.

6. Deep inside your ears are semicircular canals.

7. These canals are filled with a fluid and are lined with special hairs.

8. These hairs pick up the sense of movement when you change position.

9. Usually, the fluid lies still in the bottom of the canals.

10. Quick, violent motions make the fluid move around the canals.

11. This can cause a sick feeling in your stomach.

Add a prepositional phrase to each sentence. Write the new sentence on the line.

12. Lying down may help you feel better.

_____

_____

13. There is less motion in the front seat, so you might move.

_____

_____

14. Reading can make motion sickness worse, so don't ever read.

_____

_____

Unit 1

Core Skills Language Arts, Grade 5

Preposition or Adverb?

Some words can be used as prepositions or adverbs.

Examples: The cat climbed *up* the tree.   We looked *up*.

Circle *preposition* or *adverb* to identify the underlined word in each sentence.

1. The Morgans were driving <u>down</u> the highway.   *preposition*   *adverb*

2. Suddenly, the youngest child cried <u>out</u>.   *preposition*   *adverb*

3. "Don't drive <u>through</u> the lake, Mom!" he shouted.   *preposition*   *adverb*

4. The family looked <u>around</u>.   *preposition*   *adverb*

5. <u>On</u> the road they saw shimmering patches of water.   *preposition*   *adverb*

6. "It's just a mirage, David," his sister Camille said, looking <u>outside</u>.   *preposition*   *adverb*

7. "No matter how far we drive, we will never even get <u>near</u> it," Camille explained.   *preposition*   *adverb*

8. "On a day like this, a hot layer of air is <u>above</u> the road," said David's mother.   *preposition*   *adverb*

9. "The hot layer of air is bending the light, as if <u>through</u> a prism," continued Camille.   *preposition*   *adverb*

Add a prepositional phrase to each sentence.

10. The family continued to drive _____.

11. _____ they decided to stop.

12. They got out _____

13. They looked _____

37

Conjunctions

A **conjunction** is a word that joins words or groups of words.

Conjunctions may be used in several ways. The conjunction *and* is used to mean "together." The conjunction *but* is used to show contrast. The conjunction *or* is used to show choice.

Examples: Patrick *and* the twins looked at their new home.
His mother felt sad, *but* Patrick was excited.
Might this old house hold mysteries *or* treasures?

Complete each sentence, using the conjunction that has the meaning in ( ).

1. The house looked bare _____ gloomy.
   (together)

2. The twins began to cry, _____ Patrick cheered them up.
   (contrast)

3. Patrick walked from room to room _____ looked for trapdoors.
   (together)

4. He did not find any trapdoors _____ mysterious stairways.
   (choice)

5. Patrick was disappointed, _____ his parents were glad.
   (contrast)

6. They did not want a house with ghosts _____ goblins in it.
   (choice)

7. Patrick told them there might be treasure _____ gold instead.
   (together)

8. His mother _____ father thought he was being silly.
   (together)

9. The treasure could be in the cellar _____ in the backyard.
   (choice)

10. He found a coin in the backyard near the cellar door, _____ he knew that he was right.
    (together)

11. People were coming to work on the house, _____ Patrick was afraid they would find the treasure first.
    (together)

12. His parents might think it was silly, _____ Patrick would not stop searching.
    (contrast)

Correlative Conjunctions

Correlative conjunctions work in pairs to join words or groups of words. They are often used to emphasize relationships between ideas.

neither...nor	either...or	not only...but also

Examples: Joella said she was *neither* tired *nor* hungry after her long walk.
(Neither condition is true.)
Neither Harvey *nor* Charlie enjoyed the concert. (No one did.)

Mr. Brown will *either* fly *or* take the train to attend his college reunion.
(He will do only one activity.)
Either David *or* Kim will complete the assignment first.
(Only one person will complete the action.)

Rae is *not only* my sister *but also* my best friend. (She is both these things.)
Not only Hank *but also* Ellie ran the race. (Both people completed the action.)

Complete each sentence with a pair of correlative conjunctions.

1. _____ Marcy _____ Fran will go to the state tournament.

2. _____ Patrice _____ Kate overslept this morning.

3. Mark is _____ a community volunteer _____ a champion chess player.

4. Leah knitted _____ a scarf _____ a pair of mittens.

5. _____ Guy _____ Martha was on our badminton team.

6. Lori says she looks forward to _____ learning Spanish _____ visiting Madrid.

7. Kit and Maggie will _____ eat chocolate _____ drink soda.

8. _____ the lions _____ the tigers were visible when we went to the zoo.

9. Kenneth wants to become _____ a surgeon _____ a veterinarian.

10. Patti read _____ 100 books _____ 50 magazines last year.

11. The pantry contains _____ macaroni _____ rice.

Interjections

An **interjection** is a word or a group of words that expresses strong feeling.

Examples: *Help*! My foot is stuck!
               Wow! How did you do that?

Circle the interjection in each item.

1. Gee! The baby is so tiny.

2. Wow! Her hands are so dainty.

3. She seems to be unhappy. Oh, dear!

4. Oh, my! What can we do to make her stop crying?

5. Good grief! That doesn't work.

6. Dad, where are you? Oops!

7. Great! Here comes Dad.

8. Alas! We cannot calm the baby. Can you help, Dad?

9. Of course! I'll show you what to do.

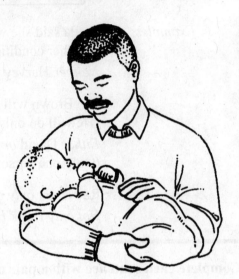

Add an interjection to each item to express strong feeling. Punctuate correctly.

10. _____ She smiled at me!

11. _____ I knew she recognized me. I'm her brother, after all.

12. _____ I think the baby is going to sneeze.

13. She already did. _____

14. _____ I just dropped the rattle.

15. _____ I hope she doesn't start crying again.

16. _____ I can't stand all this noise!

17. _____ When will we get some peace and quiet around here?

18. That will happen after she leaves for college. _____

Name _____   Date _____

What Is a Sentence?

A **sentence** is a group of words that expresses a complete thought. It always begins with a capital letter. It always ends with a punctuation mark.

Every sentence has two parts. The **subject** is the part about which something is being said. The **predicate** tells about the subject.

Subject	Predicate
My fifth-grade class	is going on a field trip.

The **complete subject** is all the words that make up the subject. A **simple subject** is the key word or words in the subject of a sentence. The simple subject tells whom or what the sentence is about.

The **complete predicate** is a word or group of words that tells something about the subject. The **simple predicate** is the key word or words in the complete predicate. The simple predicate is an action verb or a linking verb, together with any helping verbs.

Examples: A long, yellow school bus is taking us to New York. (complete subject)
A long, yellow school bus is taking us to New York. (simple subject)
Our teacher sat up front. (complete predicate)
Our teacher sat up front. (simple predicate)

Add a complete subject or a complete predicate to each sentence.

1. Mr. and Mrs. Brown _____.

2. _____ got off the bus in New York.

3. Tall buildings _____.

4. Some students _____.

5. The field trip _____.

6. _____ wants to go again soon.

7. Next time, the adults _____.

8. Before the second trip, they _____.

9. _____ will make the trip a success.

Unit 2
Core Skills Language Arts, Grade 5

Is It a Sentence?

> Remember that a sentence is a group of words that expresses a complete thought. It always begins with a capital letter. It always ends with a punctuation mark.
>
> *Example:*   The capital of Illinois is Springfield.

If a group of words is a sentence, write it correctly. Capitalize the first word, and end the sentence with a period. If the group is not a sentence, write *not a sentence*.

1. we memorized the capitals of all of the states

_____

2. everyone knew the capital of Arkansas

_____

3. the capital is not always the largest city in the state

_____

4. you should picture the map in your mind

_____

5. the left side is the west side

_____

6. right through the middle of the country

_____

7. that river empties into the Gulf of Mexico

_____

8. the Hudson River valley in New York

_____

Subjects and Predicates

Be sure your sentences have two parts, a **subject** and a **predicate**. The subject is the part about which something is being said. The predicate tells about the subject.

Subject   **Predicate**
My whole family   went to the mall.

Which sentence part is missing? Write *subject* or *predicate* on the line.

1. Your eyes _____.

2. Your other sense organs _____.

3. _____ pick up sounds.

4. _____ feel hot and cold.

5. The tongue _____.

Read each sentence. Underline the subject. Circle the predicate.

6. The eye is made of many parts.

7. The pupil is the round, black center of the eye.

8. The outer, colored part is called the iris.

9. The iris is made of a ring of muscle.

10. Too much light can damage the eye.

11. The iris closes up in bright light.

12. Some people are colorblind.

13. They cannot see shades of red and green.

14. A nearsighted person cannot see distant things well.

15. Close objects are blurry to a farsighted person.

16. Farsighted people often use reading glasses.

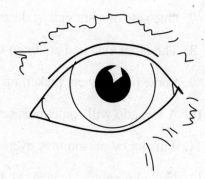

Simple Subjects and Complete Subjects

> Remember that the simple subject is the main word or words in the complete subject of a sentence. The complete subject includes all the words that tell whom or what the sentence is about.
>
> *Examples:*   The county's <u>fair</u> was the best ever this year. (simple subject)
> <u>The games on the midway</u> had good prizes. (complete subject)

Read each sentence. Underline the complete subject. Then, write the simple subject on the line.

1. Two young men were on their way from Dallas to Waco, Texas. _____

2. A raging tornado was also on its way to Waco. _____

3. Two square miles of the city would soon be twisted and destroyed. _____

4. An odd roaring noise began with the rain. _____

5. The strong wind tore buildings apart. _____

6. Giant walls fell into the street. _____

7. One side of a street was destroyed in Waco. _____

8. The other side had not been touched. _____

9. Some people were picked up by the wind. _____

10. A tornado will sometimes set a person down gently. _____

11. This lucky person may even be unhurt. _____

12. Unlucky people may be set down violently by a tornado. _____

13. Dorothy was among the lucky ones. _____

14. She was set down safely in Oz. _____

15. A ride in a tornado would be quite an experience. _____

Compound Subjects

A **compound subject** is two or more simple subjects that have the same predicate.

Join the two or more simple subjects in a compound subject with *and* or *or*.

Examples: Bright <u>sun</u> *and* <u>expanses</u> of sand make Hawaii a popular vacation spot.

           <u>Surfing</u> *or* <u>swimming</u> can be done on the famous beaches.

Read each sentence. Write the simple subjects that make up the compound subject and write the joining word.

1. Sally and John like to take care of their garden.

_____

2. Roses, daisies, and violets are their favorite flowers.

_____

3. Jim and Meg came over for lunch in the garden.

_____

4. Sally, John, Jim, and Meg sat under the big apple tree.

_____

5. A picnic basket and a jug of lemonade were placed on the blanket.

_____

6. The four friends and their two dogs had a wonderful afternoon.

_____

7. Apples, peaches, and plums were served for dessert.

_____

8. Frankie and Joanne brought some movies over later.

_____

9. The six friends, the two dogs, and a few cats went inside after sunset.

_____

Simple Predicates and Complete Predicates

The **simple predicate** is the main word or words in the complete predicate of a sentence.

The **complete predicate** includes all the words that tell what the subject of the sentence is or does.

To locate the simple predicate, find the key word in the complete predicate.

Examples: Tall, snowcapped mountains <u>reach</u> high into the sky. (simple predicate)

Tall, snowcapped mountains <u>reach high into the sky</u>. (complete predicate)

Read each sentence. Underline the complete predicate. Then, write the simple predicate on the line.

1. Insects can be very interesting. _____

2. Scientists have found almost a million different types of insects. _____

3. Insects live almost everywhere on Earth's surface. _____

4. You can study insects in the woods, streams, parks, and your own yard. _____

5. An insect has no backbone. _____

6. This makes insects different from many animals. _____

7. All insects have six legs. _____

8. The first insects appeared about 400 million years ago. _____

9. Some kinds of insects live together in large groups. _____

10. Some plants capture insects and other small animals. _____

11. These kinds of plants use the insects for food. _____

12. The pitcher plant attracts insects with its sweet nectar. _____

13. The Venus flytrap snaps its leaves shut on insects. _____

14. The sundew plant traps insects with a sticky liquid. _____

Compound Predicates

> A **compound predicate** is two or more predicates that have the same subject.
>
> The simple predicates in a compound predicate are usually joined by *and* or *or*.
>
> *Examples:*   A leopard <u>sprawls</u> along a limb *and* <u>relaxes</u> in a tree.
>
> Bears <u>chase</u> *or* <u>injure</u> sheep sometimes.

Read each sentence. Write the simple predicates that make up the compound predicate and write the joining word.

1. Sandra planned and prepared a surprise party for her sister, Susie.

   _____

2. She shopped, cleaned, and cooked the day before the party.

   _____

3. She hired a clown and bought some balloons about a week ahead of time.

   _____

4. Four days before the party, Sandra ordered a cake and borrowed extra plates.

   _____

5. The guests wore party hats and played party games.

   _____

6. Everyone ate, laughed, and danced.

   _____

7. Some of the children cleared the table and helped with the dishes.

   _____

8. After the party, the guests walked, ran, or rode home.

   _____

9. After the party, Sandra sat and rested.

   _____

Complete and Simple Subjects and Predicates

Remember that the complete subject includes all the words that tell whom or what the sentence is about. The simple subject is the main word or words in the complete subject.

The complete predicate includes all the words that tell what the subject of the sentence is or does. The simple predicate is the main word or words in the complete predicate.

Underline each complete subject, and circle each complete predicate. Then, write the simple subject and the simple predicate.

1. Our favorite coach cheers during the race.

   _____

2. My youngest sister swims ahead of the others.

   _____

3. Her strokes cut through the water.

   _____

4. Ripples splash at the edge of the pool.

   _____

5. The exciting race ends with a surprise.

   _____

6. My sister's team finishes first.

   _____

7. The people in the bleachers cheer wildly.

   _____

8. The team holds the silver trophy for a school photograph.

   _____

9. The team members hug each other happily.

   _____

Simple and Compound Sentences

A sentence that expresses only one complete thought is a **simple sentence**.

A **compound sentence** is made up of two or more simple sentences joined by a conjunction such as *and, or,* or *but*. Use a comma (,) before a conjunction that joins two sentences.

Examples: The family moved to Ohio. (simple sentence)
Patrick liked his new house, and he decided to explore. (compound sentence)

Read each sentence. Underline each simple subject. Circle each simple predicate. Then, write whether each sentence is a *simple sentence* or a *compound sentence*.

1. Once the house was part of the Underground Railroad, and it had many hiding places.

_____

2. Between 1830 and 1860, the Underground Railroad brought about 50,000 slaves to freedom.

_____

3. Farm wagons were the "trains" on this railroad.

_____

4. Often, the "train rides" were long walks between stations.

_____

5. Runaway slaves stopped at "stations" along the way, but they rarely stayed for long.

_____

6. The home of Frederick Douglass was one "station" on the track to freedom.

_____

7. Levi Coffin was a "conductor" in Indiana, and he earned the title "President of the Underground Railroad."

_____

8. Dies Drear was also a "conductor," but he lived in Ohio.

_____

9. Allan Pinkerton made barrels in Illinois, but he also hid slaves in his shop.

_____

10. Harriet Tubman led slaves to the North, and sometimes she took them to Canada.

_____

Kinds of Sentences

A **declarative sentence** makes a statement or tells something. It ends with a period (.).

An **interrogative sentence** asks a question. It ends with a question mark (?).

An **imperative sentence** makes a request or gives a command. It ends with a period (.). *You* (understood) is the subject of an imperative sentence: (You) Look how big it is.

An **exclamatory sentence** shows strong feeling or surprise. It ends with an exclamation point (!).

Examples: We are going to see the Statue of Liberty. (declarative)
Have you ever seen it? (interrogative)
Come see it with me. (imperative)
It must be very heavy! (exclamatory)

End each sentence with the correct punctuation mark. Then, write whether the sentence is declarative, interrogative, imperative, or exclamatory.

1. We are going to New York to see the Statue of Liberty _____

2. We have studied about it in school _____

3. Have you ever seen the Statue of Liberty _____

4. What a feeling it is to be close to her _____

5. Stand over there and pose for a photo _____

6. It is difficult to imagine that she was a gift _____

7. Can you imagine getting such a large gift _____

8. It would take many mail trucks to deliver it _____

9. We enjoyed our trip to New York this year _____

10. Please go if you ever get the chance _____

11. Did you know that many New Yorkers have never visited the statue _____

12. Don't be one of those people _____

Subjects in Imperative Sentences

> Remember that in an imperative sentence, *you* is always the subject. Often, the word *you* does not appear in the sentence. It is said to be "understood."
>
> *Example:*   (*You*) Read the directions carefully.

Read each sentence. Circle the number before each imperative sentence. On the line, write the simple subject of each sentence.

1. Trash is one of our biggest problems. _____

2. Be very careful with empty cans and bottles. _____

3. Don't just toss them out. _____

4. Put cans and bottles in separate bags. _____

5. The trash problem can be solved. _____

6. Take old newspapers to recycling centers. _____

7. Never toss plastic trash on the ground. _____

8. Pieces of plastic can kill animals. _____

Change each declarative sentence to an imperative sentence. Write the new sentence on the line.

9. Packages with too much wrapping should be avoided.

_____

10. People should buy the largest sizes of products.

_____

11. Old T-shirts can be used as wiping rags.

_____

12. Both sides of writing paper can be used.

_____

Agreement of Subjects and Verbs

A verb must agree with its subject in number. Use a singular verb with a singular subject. Use a plural verb with a plural subject or with a compound subject joined by *and*.

Examples: *Chad finds* a magic carpet. (singular)
                       It flies through the air. (singular)
                       They have fun. (plural)
                       He and his friends ride the carpet. (plural)

Underline the simple subject of each sentence. Then, complete each sentence correctly by circling the form of the verb in ( ) that agrees with the subject.

1. Chad and his friends (look, looks) around in the old house.

2. Chad (find, finds) an old rug rolled up in a corner.

3. He (pull, pulls) it out and unrolls it.

4. The rug (take, takes) Chad for a ride around the room.

5. Chad's friends (come, comes) into the room as the carpet lands.

6. They (stand, stands) staring with their mouths open.

7. Then, Chad (explain, explains) the magic powers of the rug.

8. The rug (seat, seats) four people.

9. Chad and his friends (go, goes) for a long ride on the rug.

10. They (fly, flies) over the town and the river.

11. Later, Chad (ride, rides) the rug to visit his aunt in the hospital.

12. The next day, he (hear, hears) his mother talking on the phone.

13. She (share, shares) good news with him.

14. His aunt (feel, feels) better and (has, have) been released from the hospital.

Combining Sentences with the Same Subject or Predicate

A good writer combines two or more sentences that have the same subject or predicate. The conjunctions *and*, *but*, and *or* are often used to combine sentence parts.

When two sentences have the same predicate, the subjects can be combined.

Example: Theseus was angry. King Minos was angry.
Theseus *and* King Minos were angry.

When two sentences have the same subject, the predicates can be combined.

Example: Theseus found the ring. Theseus returned it.
Theseus found the ring *and* returned it.

How to Combine Sentences with the Same Subjects or Predicates

1. Find two or more sentences that have the same subject or predicate.

2. Combine the subjects or predicates with the joining word that most clearly expresses your meaning to the audience.

3. If you combine subjects, make sure you use the plural form of the verb.

Rewrite this paragraph. Combine sentences with the same subjects or predicates to make it more interesting to read.

Each year, Mrs. Martinez teaches a Greek mythology unit. Mr. Gibson teaches a Greek mythology unit. They ask students to name their favorite Greek gods. They ask students to name their favorite Greek goddesses. Zeus is always on the list. Athena is always on the list.

_____

_____

_____

_____

_____

_____

_____

Combining Adjectives and Adverbs in Sentences

To avoid short, choppy sentences, a writer often combines two or more sentences that describe the same subject. Sentences that describe the same subject with different adjectives can sometimes be combined.

Example: Joanie was *diligent*. She was also *courageous*.
Joanie was *diligent and courageous*.

Sentences that describe the same verb with different adverbs can also be combined.

Example: Joanie studied *eagerly*. She studied *carefully*.
Joanie studied *eagerly and carefully*.

How to Combine Sentences with Adjectives and Adverbs

1. Look for different adjectives or adverbs that describe the same subject or verb.

2. Use an appropriate conjunction (*and*, *but*, or *or*) to combine the adjectives or adverbs.

3. If you combine three or more adjectives or adverbs in one sentence, use commas to separate them.

Combine each set of sentences to make one sentence. Then, write if you combined adjectives or adverbs.

1. Joanie waited patiently. She waited quietly. _____

_____

2. She had felt disappointed before. She had felt rejected before. _____

_____

3. She really wanted to be a scientist. She truly wanted to be a scientist. _____

_____

4. Joanie read the letter slowly. She read the letter calmly. _____

_____

Joining Sentences

A writer can join two short, choppy sentences into one that is more interesting to read. The result is a compound sentence.

Use the conjunction *and* to join two sentences that show addition or similarity.

Example: Patrick saw the house. He decided it was haunted.
                Patrick saw the house, *and* he decided it was haunted.

Use the conjunction *but* to join two sentences that show contrast.

Example: Patrick ran up the steps. He stopped at the door.
                Patrick ran up the steps, *but* he stopped at the door.

Use the conjunction *or* to join two sentences that show choice.

Example: Should he go inside? Should he explore outside?
                Should he go inside, *or* should he explore outside?

How to Combine Sentences into Compound Sentences

1. Choose two short sentences you want to combine.

2. Select the appropriate conjunction to combine them.

3. Be sure the conjunction makes the meaning of the combined sentence clear.

4. Put a comma before the conjunction.

Join each pair of sentences. Use the conjunction *and, but,* or *or*.

1. Patrick studied the wall. He found a hidden button.

_____

2. Patrick pushed the button. The bookcase moved.

_____

3. Patrick could wait. He could explore the path.

_____

4. He wasn't afraid. He wasn't comfortable, either.

_____

Sentence Variety

> To add variety to sentences, a writer sometimes changes the order of the words. Usually the subject comes before the verb. This is called **natural order**.
>
> *Example:*   Margaret led Danny down a twisting path.
>
> Sometimes the subject and verb can be reversed. This is called **inverted order**.
>
> *Example:*   At the end of the path was a small shack.

How to Vary Word Order in Sentences

1. Choose a sentence you have written in which the subject and the verb can be reversed.

2. Write the sentence in inverted order. Be sure the meaning of the sentence does not change.

Write each sentence, changing the word order whenever it would not change the meaning. Tell which sentences cannot be changed and explain why.

1. On the little door shone the sunlight.

_____

2. Margaret and Danny walked into the shack.

_____

3. Inside the shack was a large wooden table.

_____

4. On the table lay a black cat.

_____

5. Margaret reached out to the cat.

_____

6. Margaret told Danny to follow her out.

_____

Avoiding Sentence Fragments and Run-on Sentences

To avoid writing **sentence fragments**, be sure each sentence has a subject and a predicate and expresses a complete thought.

To avoid writing **run-on sentences**, be sure you join two complete sentences with a comma and a conjunction. You may also write them as two separate sentences.

Read each group of words. If it is a simple sentence, write *simple sentence* on the line. If it is a sentence fragment or a run-on sentence, rewrite it correctly.

1. A box turtle is a reptile it lives in woods and fields.

_____

2. The box turtle has a hinged lower shell.

_____

3. Can pull its legs, head, and tail inside its shell and get "boxed in."

_____

4. Many kinds of turtles on land and in the water.

_____

5. Belong to the same family as lizards, snakes, alligators, and crocodiles.

_____

_____

6. Box turtles will eat earthworms, insects, berries, and green leafy vegetables.

_____

_____

7. Painted turtles eat mealworms, earthworms, minnows, and insects the musk turtle finds food along the bottoms of ponds or streams.

_____

_____

Correcting Run-on Sentences

> Good writers avoid run-on sentences. Run-on sentences may be rewritten as simple sentences or as compound sentences.

Read each run-on sentence. Fix it in two ways. Write two simple sentences, and write one compound sentence.

1. You'll need 101 index cards you'll need a colored marker.

   a. _____

   b. _____

2. Print the name of a state or a state capital on each index card print the rules on the last index card.

   a. _____

   _____

   b. _____

   _____

3. Put the marker away put all the cards in an envelope.

   a. _____

   b. _____

4. This game is for small groups up to three students may play.

   a. _____

   b. _____

5. Players mix up the cards they lay the cards facedown.

   a. _____

   b. _____

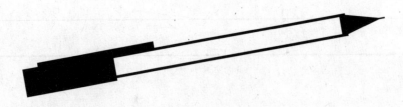

Capitalization of Names and Titles

Begin each part of the name of a person with a capital letter. Capitalize an initial used in a name.

Begin a title of a person, such as *Ms., Mrs., Mr.,* or *Dr.,* with a capital letter.

Always capitalize the word *I.*

Examples: Pete P. Pelky
Mrs. Morrow
Michael Mixx and I went camping.

Read each sentence. Circle the letters that should be capital letters.

1. i was going camping with my friend michael.

2. We met mr. carl g. carbur at the camping supply store.

3. michael and i decided that we needed a new tent.

4. mrs. albright showed us many different tents.

5. we chose one just like dr. pelky's.

6. michael's mother, mrs. mixx, gave us a ride to the campsite.

7. After we set up the tent, i walked down the road.

8. dr. pelky was at the next site!

9. dr. pelky was camping with mario j. moreno.

10. mario showed michael and me a great place to fish.

11. i caught some trout, and michael caught a bass.

12. michael and i ate supper at dr. pelky's camp.

Capitalization of Proper Nouns and Proper Adjectives

Remember that a proper noun names a particular person, place, holiday, day of the week, or month. A proper adjective is formed from a proper noun.

Capitalize the first letter of each important word in a proper noun or proper adjective.

Examples: Canada   Fourth of July   Wednesday   German shepherd

Rewrite each sentence, using capital letters where needed.

1. My best friends and I plan to tour the united states.

_____

2. My friend sandy is very excited because she has never been to california.

_____

_____

3. She has never tasted any mexican food, either.

_____

4. She will be coming from new york and meeting jane in philadelphia.

_____

5. Then, the two of them will pick up roxanne in phoenix, arizona.

_____

6. When they get to san francisco, we will all go out for chinese food.

_____

_____

7. If we go to green's restaurant for vegetarian food, even jane will like the brussels sprouts.

_____

_____

Using Capital Letters

Use a capital letter to begin the first word of a sentence.

Begin each important word in the name of a town, city, state, province, or country with a capital letter.

Begin each important word in the names of streets and their abbreviations with capital letters.

Begin the name of a day of the week or its abbreviation with a capital letter.

Begin the name of a month or its abbreviation with a capital letter.

Examples: Detroit, Michigan
Athens, Greece
Golden Gate Avenue or Ave.
Saturday or Sat.
November or Nov.

Rewrite each sentence. Add capital letters where they are needed.

1. i found a book of rhymes at the library in milwaukee.

_____

2. the book was published in london, england.

_____

3. the book contained rhymes from the countries of kenya, ecuador, and even new zealand.

_____

_____

4. my favorite poem told of a crocodile who lived at the corner of cricket court and bee boulevard.

_____

_____

5. we decided to drive to the rocky mountains on sunday.

_____

6. we finally reached el paso, texas, on tuesday.

_____

_____

Periods

Use a **period** (.) at the end of a declarative or imperative sentence.

Use a period after an abbreviation.

Use a period after an initial.

Use a period after the numeral in a main topic and after the capital letter in a subtopic of an outline.

Examples: Arithmetic adds up to answers.
U.S.   Fri.   Jan.   Dr.   A.M.   Blvd.
Capt. Chou A. Hak-Tak

I. How to Master Multiplication
    A. Learn multiplication tables
    B. Practice doing multiplication problems

Correct each item. Add periods where they are needed.

1. Last week our class visited a Chinese exhibit

2. I thought the pen-and-brush pictures were beautiful

3. I was also impressed with the carved jade ships

4. Our teacher, Ms Garrett, showed us a book about Chinese paintings in the museum gift shop

5. The book was written by Dr Chun B Fong.

6. Dr Fong included a chapter about wood-block prints.

7. Our guide, T R Adams, knew all about Chinese art

8. J B Barnard asked several questions.

9. The museum is located on N Clark St

10. I Crafts from China
    A Silk painting
    B Porcelain

Abbreviations and Initials

An **abbreviation** is a short way of writing a word or words.

Begin abbreviations with a capital letter. End most abbreviations with a period.

An **initial** is an abbreviation of a name. The initial is the first letter of the name.

Use capital letters and periods to write an initial.

Examples: Doctor = *Dr.*   Road = *Rd.*   Tuesday = *Tues.*
              August = *Aug.*   Tina Devers = *T. Devers*

Rewrite each item. Use the correct abbreviations and initials for the underlined words.

1. My name is <u>Chester Michael</u> Dooley. I live at 4338 Market <u>Boulevard</u> in Alabaster, Alabama. My birthday is on <u>October</u> 27.

_____

_____

2. Suzy <u>Elizabeth</u> Ziegler requests the pleasure of your company at a party in honor of her friend, Maryanne <u>Margaret</u> Marbles. Please come to the country club at 23 Country Club <u>Drive</u> at 4:00 <u>in the afternoon</u> on <u>Tuesday</u>, <u>April</u> 14.

_____

_____

_____

3. The <u>James Harold</u> Calabases take great pride in announcing the birth of their twins, Heather <u>Holly</u> Calabas and <u>James Harold</u> Calabas, <u>Junior</u>. This happy event took place on <u>Monday</u>, <u>August</u> 23, at 3:00 <u>in the morning</u>.

_____

_____

_____

4. <u>Fortunato Augustus</u> Jones has been appointed assistant to the president of Bags and Boxes, <u>Incorporated</u>. This store is located at 45 Ninety-ninth <u>Avenue</u>.

_____

_____

Using Commas in Sentences

Use a **comma (,)** after the words *yes* and *no* when they begin a statement.

Use commas to separate three or more words in a series.

Use a comma before the word *and, but,* or *or* when two sentences are combined.

Use a comma to separate a word used in direct address from a sentence.

Use a comma between a quotation and the rest of the sentence.

Examples: *Yes,* the boys should join their father.
The boys ran *quickly, silently, and anxiously.*
Josh felt tired, *but* he continued to run.
"Andy, I need to rest for a minute."
"We are almost there," said Andy.

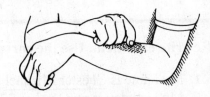

Rewrite each sentence, adding commas where they are needed.

1. Three plants to avoid are poison ivy poison oak and poison sumac.

   _____

2. Steven I see that you have some poison oak growing in your yard.

   _____

3. "Your dog cat or rabbit can pick it up on its fur and rub against you" Wesley said.

   _____

4. Yes it will make your skin burn itch and swell.

   _____

5. Dana put his clothes in a hamper and his mother got a rash from touching the clothes.

   _____

Cross out any commas that are incorrect. Rewrite the sentence on the line, adding any commas that are needed.

6. Poison ivy looks like, a shrub a vine, or a small plant.

   _____

7. Poison ivy, has green leaves in clusters of three and so does poison oak.

   _____

Use a comma before the word *and, but,* or *or* in a compound sentence.

Use a comma after time-order words, such as *first, next, then,* and *last.*

Use a comma after introductory words and phrases.

Use a comma to separate three or more words in a series.

Examples: The old house was big, *and* it also looked mysterious.
First, I decided to explore the house.
Before very long, I found a tunnel.
The tunnel was *dark, damp, and long.*

Correct each sentence. Put commas where they are needed.

1. The old house looked interesting but it also looked frightening.

2. I inspected the upstairs and I looked in the backyard.

3. The cellar door was open and I decided to look inside.

4. I could look around in one room or I could go to another room.

5. First I was worried that there was something in the cellar.

6. Next I thought I heard voices coming from the other room.

7. After a while I decided I had better get out of the cellar.

8. In addition I began to remember the stories my mother had told me.

9. I thought of all the other people who had lived played and worked in this house.

10. I imagined that I heard footsteps whispers and singing.

11. I ran out of the cellar and I closed the door behind me.

12. Soon I decided I wanted to explore the upstairs of the house.

More Uses for Commas

Use a comma in an address to separate the city and state or the city and country.

Use a comma between the day and the year.

Use a comma after the greeting of a friendly letter and after the closing of any letter.

Examples: Albuquerque, New Mexico   Lima, Peru
April 30, 2013   Monday, January 28, 2013
Dear Uncle Ernie,
Yours truly,

Correct each letter. Add commas where they are needed.

732 Cactus Road
Albuquerque NM 87107
April 22 2013

Dear Ernest

    I need to show Father that I am old enough to go on the summer trail drive. Please help me by reminding Father that I have helped you do many things this year. I will appreciate any help that you can give me.

Your friend

David Ortez

441 Scorpion Trail
Albuquerque NM 87112
May 3 2013

Dear David

    You have helped me a great deal during this past year. I will speak to your father. Remember that your father is a fair man, and he will reward you when he thinks you are ready.

Sincerely

Ernest

Question Marks and Exclamation Points

> Use a **question mark (?)** at the end of an interrogative sentence.
>
> Use an **exclamation point (!)** at the end of an exclamatory sentence.
>
> *Examples:*   Did Mika know what was in the box?
>
> What a surprise she received when she reached inside!

Finish each sentence with a question mark or an exclamation point.

1. Did you know that our teacher, Mr. Holder, visited China last month

2. What a wonderful adventure he had

3. Look at the wonderful postcards he sent our class

4. Do you know where he stayed

5. When did Mr. Holder return

6. Could you tell us about his trip

7. He found a pearl in an oyster shell

8. That was a lucky find

9. You should see the beautiful photographs Mr. Holder took

10. What kind of camera did he use

11. It really is a good one

12. What did he bring back

13. What a beautiful necklace that is

14. Did you know that jade is very expensive

15. Mrs. Holder will certainly be surprised

16. Did Mr. Holder visit the Great Wall of China

17. Of course he did

18. What an awesome sight that must have been

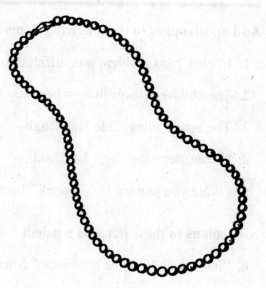

Apostrophes and Colons

> Use an **apostrophe (')** to show that one or more letters have been left out in a contraction.
>
> To form a singular possessive noun, add an apostrophe and *s* to singular nouns.
>
> To form a plural possessive noun, add an apostrophe to a plural noun that ends in *s*.
>
> Add an apostrophe and *s* to plural nouns that do not end in *s* to show possession.
>
> Use a **colon (:)** between the hour and the minute in the time of day.
>
> Use a colon after the greeting in a business letter.
>
> | *Examples:* | was not = *wasn't* | could not = *couldn't* |
> | --- | --- | --- |
> | | *Jane's* father | the *pig's* tail |
> | | *guests'* laughter | the *maids'* voices |
> | | the *children's* adventure | the *men's* story |
> | | 2:25 P.M. | 5:13 A.M. |
> | | Dear Ms. Parker: | Dear Sir or Madam: |

Add apostrophes to the following items as needed.

1. Uncle Chens problem was difficult to explain.

2. The childrens faces lit up when they saw him flying.

3. The boys smiles made Jane laugh.

4. "I cant stop laughing," Jane said.

5. "Wont you join us, Ms. Parker?" Jane asked.

Add colons to these items as needed.

6. "It's only 3 30 in the afternoon," Michel said.

7. "We can stay until 6 00," Meri replied.

8. The movie starts at 7 15.

9. Dear Ms. Parker

   Your application for employment has been received.

Contractions

A **contraction** is a short way of writing two words together. Some of the letters are left out. An apostrophe takes the place of the missing letters.

Examples: she + will = *she'll*   had + not = *hadn't*   I + would = *I'd*

Rewrite each sentence. Replace the underlined words with a contraction.

1. <u>You are</u> getting very hot in this summer weather.

   _____

2. Do you think <u>you would</u> like a water slide?

   _____

3. <u>You will</u> need some plastic at least ten feet long.

   _____

4. <u>It is</u> best to get heavy plastic.

   _____

5. That way, it <u>will not</u> tear too easily.

   _____

6. Place the plastic on a grassy spot where there <u>are not</u> any bumps.

   _____

7. You can use stones to hold the plastic down, but they <u>must not</u> be sharp.

   _____

8. If you <u>do not</u> have a sprinkler, get one.

   _____

9. You <u>should not</u> put the sprinkler too far from the plastic.

   _____

10. You <u>must not</u> let the plastic get dry.

   _____

Direct Quotations and Dialogue

Use a **direct quotation** to tell a speaker's exact words.

Use **quotation marks (" ")** before and after the words a speaker says.

Begin the first word a speaker says with a capital letter. Put end punctuation before the ending quotation marks. Begin a new paragraph each time the speaker changes.

If the quotation is interrupted by other words, place quotation marks around the exact spoken words only.

Examples: Dad asked, "Where have you been?"
"I went to the store," Vic said. "Then, I went to the library."

Write quotation marks where they are needed in the following sentences.

1. Have you heard of the Nobel Peace Prize? asked Emi.

2. Yes. Mother Teresa and Nelson Mandela have won it, replied Jan.

3. But do you know who Nobel was? Emi asked.

4. Jan responded, No, I guess I don't.

5. He invented dynamite, stated Emi.

6. It seems weird, said Jan, to name a peace prize for the inventor of dynamite.

7. In fact, Emi said, dynamite was once called Nobel's Safety Blasting Powder.

8. Nobel patented the blasting powder in 1867, Emi continued.

9. He did not want dynamite used for war, he said.

10. He added, Nobel once said that war is the horror of horrors and the greatest of all crimes.

11. How did the Nobel Prizes get started? asked Jan.

12. Emi said, In his will, Nobel said that his money should be used to establish prizes in five areas: physics, chemistry, medicine, literature, and peace.

13. Sometimes a prize is shared by two or three people, he continued.

14. I'd like to know more about some of the winners, Jan said.

15. Jimmy Carter, 39th President of the United States, won the Nobel Peace Prize in 2002, replied Emi.

Titles

Underline the titles of books, newspapers, magazines, movies, and television shows. If you are using a computer to write, replace underlining with italics.

Use quotation marks around the titles of stories, magazine articles, essays, songs, or poems.

Begin the first word, last word, and all other important words in a title with a capital letter.

Examples: <u>All About Everything</u> (book)
<u>Shrek</u> (movie)
"Wind in the Treetops" (story)
"The Bells" (poem)

Write each title. Use capital letters correctly. Underline or use quotation marks as needed. Write *I* by the titles that would need italics when using a computer.

1. a wrinkle in time (book) _____

2. camping in the mountains (magazine article) _____

3. it's not easy being green (song) _____

4. sounder (movie) _____

5. the new york times (newspaper) _____

6. humpty dumpty (magazine) _____

7. the little house (story) _____

8. why i like gymnastics (essay) _____

9. the little prince (book) _____

10. the owl and the pussycat (poem) _____

Rewrite each sentence correctly. Write *I* by the titles that would need italics when using a computer.

11. The sixth chapter in that book is called Animal Language.

_____

_____

12. A book I really like is If I Were in Charge of the World by Judith Viorst.

_____

_____

Compound Words

A **compound word** consists of two or more words used as a single word.

A **closed compound** is a compound made of two words written together as one.
Examples: runway bookmark rainbow

An **open compound** is a compound in which the words are written separately.
Examples: dead end punching bag bean sprout

A **hyphenated compound** is a compound connected by hyphens.
Examples: father-in-law half-truth narrow-minded

There are eighteen compounds in the following sentences, but all of them are spelled incorrectly. Identify each compound, and spell it correctly. Use a dictionary if necessary. Then, write each word correctly.

1. My cousin Danielle had her wisdom-teeth pulled. _____

2. As she sat in an arm chair in the sun-shine, she thought about an old family story.

_____

3. Isaac, a ten year-old boy, had escaped from slavery. _____

4. His spirits soared skyhigh as he left his birth place. _____

5. The slavedriver went after him with blood-hounds. _____

6. Isaac hid in a stormcellar and a smoke house as he headed north to freedom.

_____

7. For three weeks he lived handtomouth, but he avoided any run ins with his former master.

_____

8. Danielle, a folk-singer of sorts, reached for her note book.

_____

9. "This is no run of the mill story," she thought as she gazed at the wall-paper.

_____

10. "This old story from our familytree will make a terrific song or even a best selling novel!"

_____

Synonyms and Antonyms

A **synonym** is a word that has almost the same meaning as another word.

When a word has several synonyms, use the one that works best in the sentence.

An **antonym** is a word that means the opposite of another word.

When a word has more than one antonym, use the one that expresses your meaning exactly.

Examples: *Jobs* is a synonym of *tasks.*
                    Short is an antonym of *tall.*

Read each sentence. Study the underlined words. Then, write *synonyms* or *antonyms* to describe the two words.

1. As Tio and Nicole approached the <u>forest</u>, they saw a path leading into the <u>woods</u>.

   _____

2. The trees were dripping with moisture, and soon Tio and Nicole's <u>dry</u> clothes were <u>soaked</u>.

   _____

3. Within the forest, the <u>upper</u> branches kept the light from reaching the <u>lower</u> levels.

   _____

4. As they walked along the muddy <u>path</u>, Tio and Nicole saw rotting leaves on the <u>trail</u>.

   _____

5. They <u>continued</u> along the trail and then <u>halted</u> suddenly in their tracks.

   _____

6. The <u>low</u> sound of a <u>soft</u> chirping had caused them to stop.

   _____

7. As they moved <u>quietly</u> through the forest, they heard a monkey <u>loudly</u> calling to other monkeys.

   _____

8. The <u>younger</u> monkeys were eating leaves of bamboo trees while the <u>older</u> ones watched.

   _____

9. One monkey was <u>curious</u> and looked at Tio and Nicole, but the others were <u>indifferent</u>.

   _____

More Synonyms and Antonyms

Remember that a synonym is a word that has almost the same meaning as another word. An antonym is a word that means the opposite of another word.

Examples: *Start* is a synonym of *begin*.
Hard is an antonym of *soft*.

Read each sentence. Identify the two words or phrases from the sentence that are antonyms, and write them on the lines.

1. Barbra had always been a success at school, but now she felt like a failure.

_____   _____

2. T.J. had been left back once because he wasn't mature enough to be promoted.

_____   _____

3. Barbra saw only one solution to her problem—she had to get rid of her report card.

_____   _____

4. Barbra had a burning feeling in her stomach that even ice-cold milk couldn't get rid of.

_____   _____

Fill in the columns of the chart with a synonym and an antonym for each of the words in the first column.

Word	Synonym	Antonym
end	_____	_____
fast	_____	_____
simple	_____	_____
gloomy	_____	_____
concealed	_____	_____
unsure	_____	_____

Prefixes

A **prefix** is a letter or group of letters added to the beginning of a root. A **root** is the simplest form of a word. Many prefixes, such as *un, im, in, re, pre, mis,* and *non,* come from Greek or Latin words.

Adding a prefix to a word changes the word's meaning.

Examples: dis + like = dislike
The boys said they *like* being in the cave.
They *dislike* the cold rocks.

Find the word in each sentence that begins with a prefix. Draw a line under the prefix. Then, write a definition of the word.

1. There may be gold in the Black Mountains, waiting to be unearthed.

   _____

2. Many people say this gold is nonexistent.

   _____

3. Others say it's there, but they are unable to find it.

   _____

4. Many searches for the gold have had to be discontinued.

   _____

5. It is improbable that any gold is there.

   _____

6. Our inability to find any probably means there is none.

   _____

On the line, write a word with the meaning given in ( ). Use one of the prefixes in the box, and use the underlined word as a root.

dis	mis	pre	re	un	non	in	im

7. I bought it last week, but I will _____ (<u>sell</u> again) it to you.

8. I have never been _____ (not <u>sincere</u>) with you.

9. I sense some _____ (opposite of <u>comfort</u>) in you.

10. Have you ever known me to _____ (<u>lead</u> incorrectly) you?

11. You don't even have to _____ (<u>pay</u> before) me for the map.

12. I'm a little _____ (not <u>organized</u>) now, but I'll get the map to you tomorrow.

Suffixes

A **suffix** is a letter or group of letters added to the ending of a root. A **root** is a word to which other word parts may be added. Many suffixes, such as *able, ible, y, ly, or, logy, ism, ment, meter,* and *en,* come from Greek or Latin words.

A suffix changes the meaning of a word.

Example: Do you get *enjoyment* from reading Greek myths, or do they *frighten* you?

Sometimes spelling changes are made when suffixes are added to roots. Drop the *e* at the end of a root before adding a suffix that begins with a vowel.

Examples: contribute—contributor   love—lovable

Noun-forming Suffixes		**Adjective-forming Suffixes**		**Verb-forming Suffixes**	
Suffix	Example	Suffix	Example	Suffix	Example
er	singer	able	laughable	en	brighten
or	director	ful	careful	ize	equalize
ness	gentleness	ible	flexible	**Adverb-forming Suffix**	
ment	appointment	ish	selfish	Suffix	Example
ism	tourism	less	careless	ly	quickly
meter	diameter	y	stormy		
logy	biology				

Add the kind of suffix given in ( ) to each word. Then, on a separate sheet of paper, write a sentence with each word you have formed.

1. sail (noun) _____

2. fear (adjective) _____

3. kind (noun) _____

4. might (adjective) _____

5. happy (noun) _____

6. light (verb) _____

7. cloud (adjective) _____

8. sudden (adverb) _____

9. quiet (adverb) _____

10. play (noun, adjective) _____

11. wonder (adjective) _____

12. teach (noun) _____

13. magnet (noun) _____

14. thermal (noun) _____

15. apology (verb) _____

16. myth (noun) _____

76

Homophones and Homographs

> **Homophones** are words that sound alike but are spelled differently and have different meanings.
>
> *Example:*   The girl *read* the *red* sign.
>
> **Homographs** are words that have the same spelling but different meanings. Some homographs are pronounced differently.
>
> *Examples:*   Some animals *live* on land and water.
>   *Live* plants are not allowed in this building.

Read each sentence. Circle the homophone in ( ) that correctly completes the sentence.

1. Leaves need (air, heir) in order to breathe.

2. If plants can't breathe, then neither can (ewe, you).

3. Of (coarse, course), if we keep cutting down trees, we'll have less oxygen.

4. It (wood, would) be a mistake to put a plant right next to a heater.

5. Most plants (need, knead) the temperature to be kept even.

6. The (main, mane) enemy of most plants is dry heat.

7. You should spray your plants with a fine (missed, mist) of warm water every day.

Use one of the following homographs to complete each sentence.

object	can	present	spring

8. If you mix your own plant food, you _____ do it in a

   _____.

9. If you _____ to putting a plant in a bigger pot, remember the

   _____ of replanting.

10. To give your crowded plant a nice _____, _____
    it with a bigger pot.

11. In the _____, many plants grow by the _____ in
    the forest.

More on Homophones

Homophones are words that sound alike. They are spelled differently and have different meanings.

Example: Brandon spent *four* days thinking about a gift *for* his friend Cara.

Complete each sentence. Choose the correct homophone in ( ). Write it on the line.

1. At the end of the _____, Brandon chose a plan.
   (week, weak)

2. He made his _____ to the bus station and traveled downtown.
   (way, weigh)

3. The sporting goods store was easy to _____.
   (fined, find)

4. Brandon thought, "I _____ what Cara would like."
   (know, no)

5. "This is what I have to _____."
   (dew, do)

6. Could he get _____ the line to get an autograph?
   (threw, through)

7. Brandon could _____ his hero.
   (see, sea)

8. His heart _____ faster.
   (beet, beat)

9. Cara would get _____ special baseball from Brandon.
   (won, one)

Write one homophone for each of the following words. Then, use five pairs of homophones correctly in sentences. Spell each homophone correctly. Use a separate sheet of paper.

10. pail _____

11. son _____

12. flea _____

13. strait _____

14. two _____

15. meet _____

16. led _____

17. sighed _____

18. blew _____

19. hymn _____

20. pane _____

21. hoarse _____

Words with Multiple Meanings

Some words have more than one meaning. When you read something, you need to be sure you know which meaning the writer intends.

Look at the words and their meanings in the chart. Then, read each sentence below, and select the appropriate meaning for the underlined word. Write it in the space provided.

Word	Meaning 1	Meaning 2
sail	cloth that catches wind to move a boat	to move in a boat
craft	a skill or an occupation	a ship, boat, or aircraft
mission	something a person sets out to do	a religious outpost
passed	moved past or went by	voted in favor of, approved
named	appointed to a job or an office	gave a name to
reached	stretched one's hand or arm out	arrived at or came to
completed	made whole with nothing missing	ended or finished

1. Ferdinand Magellan was the first explorer to <u>sail</u> around the world.

   In this sentence, *sail* means _____.

2. His <u>craft</u> had to travel from Spain across the Atlantic to South America.

   In this sentence, *craft* means _____.

3. From there his <u>mission</u> was to sail along the eastern shore until he reached the southernmost tip.

   In this sentence, *mission* means _____.

4. Magellan <u>passed</u> through a strait now named for him and found a great ocean.

   In this sentence, *passed* means _____.

5. He <u>named</u> this great ocean the Pacific Ocean, which means "peaceful ocean."

   In this sentence, *named* means _____.

6. Magellan continued sailing across the Pacific Ocean and <u>reached</u> the Philippine Islands.

   In this sentence, *reached* means _____.

7. After Magellan's death, his crew sailed on and <u>completed</u> the historic voyage around the world.

   In this sentence, *completed* means _____.

Context Clues

When you are reading, you may not know every word. If you come across a word you don't know, look at the words around it to determine its meaning. These words are called **context**. When you think you have figured out a word's meaning, you can check a dictionary to see if you are right.

Example: Raul's uncle is studying to become a U.S. <u>citizen</u>. He must learn facts about the *United States* and how its *government* works. One day he will be able to *vote*. (The context clues *United States*, *government*, and *vote* tell you that being a citizen has something to do with becoming an official member of a country. The dictionary definition of *citizen* is "a person who legally belongs to a country and has the rights and protections of that country.")

Use context clues to determine the meaning of each underlined word below. Write your own definition of each word, and then check a dictionary to see if you are right.

1. My uncle works in the <u>textile</u> industry. His factory produces cotton shirts and pants.

   _____

2. The school band played a <u>medley</u> of popular songs. Just when I recognized one tune, they started another. _____

3. Lacey took a <u>survey</u> to find out students' favorite fruit. She asked questions of people as they entered the cafeteria. _____

4. Have you ever tried to <u>assemble</u> a model airplane? It helps to read the directions before gluing all those small parts together! _____

5. Jade was <u>reluctant</u> to walk onto the stage. She was afraid she would forget the words to her speech. Slowly she walked toward the microphone, knees trembling. _____

6. Pat's mother is a <u>physician</u>. She sees sick children and tries to make them well with medicine.

   _____

7. My favorite summer activity is to <u>recline</u> on a lawn chair and nap in the warm sun.

   _____

8. Aunt Marge said the supply of fresh peaches was <u>adequate</u> to make jam. We had enough fruit to make ten quarts. _____

Troublesome Words

Use *too* when you mean "very" or "also." Use *to* when you mean "in the direction of." Use *two* when you mean the numeral 2.

Use *it's* when you mean "it is." Use *its* when you mean "belonging to it."

Use *their* when you mean "belonging to them." Use *there* when you mean "in that place." Use *they're* when you mean "they are."

Use *your* when you mean "belonging to you." Use *you're* when you mean "you are."

The word *good* is an adjective. Use *good* to describe a noun. Use *well* as an adjective when you mean "healthy." Use *well* as an adverb when you tell how something is done.

Circle the word in ( ) that correctly completes each sentence.

1. We went (to, too, two) the aquarium.

2. Len stayed home because he did not feel (good, well).

3. (Its, It's) a great place to visit.

4. You forgot to bring (you're, your) lunch.

5. (To, Too, Two) beluga whales were (there, their, they're).

6. One whale had a cute spot on (its, it's) face.

7. (You're, Your) the first person I told about our trip.

8. I wish you had been able to come, (to, too, two).

9. It was a (good, well) idea to take the trip.

10. (There, Their, They're) very happy to have students visit them.

11. The fish and other sea animals are taken care of (good, well).

12. We saw the sea otters eat (there, their, they're) meal.

13. I think (its, it's) worthwhile to go again.

14. Did you see the (to, too, two) walruses?

15. (There, Their, They're) sea lions, not walruses.

Negatives

A **negative** is a word that means "no" or "not."

The words *never, no, nobody, none, not, nothing,* and *nowhere* are negatives.

The negative word *not* is often used in contractions.

Do not use two negatives in the same sentence.

Examples: Jack had *never* worked in a store before.
           Nobody there knew him.
           He *didn't* know at first what he should do.

Complete each sentence by choosing the correct word in ( ). Avoid using two negatives in the same sentence.

1. Most people _____ never get a snakebite.
                (will, won't)

2. If you do get bitten, don't go into _____ panic.
                                  (a, no)

3. Remember that not all snakes _____ poisonous.
                             (are, aren't)

4. It's best not to do _____ that will speed the spread of the poison.
               (anything, nothing)

5. Didn't _____ in our group ever study this before?
            (anybody, nobody)

6. If you must go for help, don't _____ run.
                  (ever, never)

7. When in snake country, don't take _____ chances.
                        (any, no)

Each sentence contains a double negative. Cut or replace at least one of the negatives. Write the sentence correctly.

8. There aren't no more than four kinds of poisonous snakes in North America.

_____

_____

9. It won't do no good to try to run away from a rattlesnake.

_____

Avoiding Wordy Language

Good writers say what they mean in as few words as possible. When you revise, cross out words that don't add to the meaning.

Example: Mari was putting on her clothes and getting ready for Chet's party. (wordy)
                Mari was dressing for Chet's party. (better)

Rewrite each sentence. Replace the words in ( ) with fewer words.

1. Our family was (putting clothes and other items in) suitcases.

   _____

2. Everyone was looking forward to (the vacation that we take every year).

   _____

3. When all the suitcases were packed, Mom (put all the suitcases in) the trunk.

   _____

4. We (pulled out of the driveway) at noon on Saturday.

   _____

5. We (made our way through the streets) to the freeway.

   _____

6. We (ended up stopping every little while) because my little brother was (not feeling very well).

   _____

7. The second day we (stopped off and went to see the sites of) historical places.

   _____

8. Everyone (really had a good time on) the rest of the trip, too.

   _____

Using Sensory Images

Good writers use sensory words that appeal to some or all of the five senses.

Example: *Cold*, *white snow* blanketed the *green pine trees* in the *quiet valley*.

Read each sentence. On the line, write each underlined word and tell the sense or senses to which it most appeals as it is used in the sentence.

1. The young swimmer was wearing a <u>blue</u> suit.

   _____

2. She dove cleanly into the <u>cool</u> water.

   _____

3. The judges wrote the scores in <u>large</u> black letters.

   _____

4. The audience let out a <u>loud</u> cheer.

   _____

5. She had been practicing so long her hair had the odor of <u>chlorine</u>.

   _____

6. One tile on the practice pool was rough and <u>jagged</u>.

   _____

7. The <u>rough</u> edge had cut her foot, and she had yelled, "Ouch!"

   _____

8. Her coach had put a <u>soft</u> bandage on it, and it was fine now.

   _____

9. The sweatshirt she put on was <u>warm</u> and soft.

   _____

10. After practice, she had a <u>delicious</u> sandwich.

    _____

84

Denotation and Connotation

The **denotation** of a word is its exact meaning as stated in a dictionary.

The **connotation** of a word is a second, suggested meaning of a word. This added meaning often suggests something positive or negative.

Examples: *Skinny* suggests "too thin." *Skinny* has a negative connotation.
                 Slender suggests "attractively thin." *Slender* has a positive connotation.

Some words are neutral. They do not suggest either good or bad meanings. For example, *hat, seventeen,* and *yearly* are neutral words.

Circle the word in ( ) that has a positive connotation.

1. Our trip to the amusement park was (good, wonderful).

2. (Brave, foolhardy) people rode on the roller coaster.

3. We saw (fascinating, weird) animals in the animal house.

4. Some of the monkeys made (hilarious, goofy) faces.

5. Everyone's face wore a (smile, smirk) on the way home.

Circle the word in ( ) that has a negative connotation.

6. We bought (cheap, inexpensive) souvenirs at the park.

7. I ate a (soggy, moist) sandwich.

8. Mike (nagged, reminded) us to go to the fun house.

9. He was very (determined, stubborn) about going.

10. The fun house was (comical, silly).

Answer the following questions.

11. Which is more serious, a <u>problem</u> or a <u>disaster</u>?

_____

12. Which is worth more, something <u>old</u> or something <u>antique</u>?

_____

The denotation of a word is its exact meaning as stated in a dictionary.

The connotation of a word is an added meaning that suggests something positive or negative.

Some words, such as *hat, seventeen,* or *yearly,* are neutral. They do not suggest either good or bad meanings.

Examples: The denotation of *stingy* is "not generous" or "miserly."
Stingy suggests "selfish." *Stingy* has a negative connotation.

Read each sentence. Write *negative* if the underlined word has a negative connotation. Write *positive* if it has a positive connotation. Write *neutral* if the word is neutral.

_____ **1.** This is my <u>house</u>.

_____ **2.** This is my <u>home</u>.

_____ **3.** Darren's friends <u>discussed</u> his problem.

_____ **4.** Darren's friends <u>gossiped</u> about his problem.

_____ **5.** Our dog is <u>sick</u>.

_____ **6.** Our dog is <u>diseased</u>.

_____ **7.** The play was <u>boring</u>.

_____ **8.** The play was <u>fantastic</u>.

_____ **9.** Angie was <u>stubborn</u>.

_____ **10.** Angie was <u>determined</u>.

Complete each sentence with a word that suggests the connotation given.

11. The gift from my aunt was _____. (positive)

12. The gift from my aunt was _____. (negative)

13. The gift from my aunt was _____. (neutral)

Using Figurative Language

Writers often use **figurative language** to compare unlike things. Figurative language uses figures of speech such as similes, metaphors, and personification. Figurative language gives a meaning that is not exactly that of the words used. Figurative language tries to create a clearer word picture for the reader.

Writers can create vivid word pictures by comparing two things that are not usually thought of as being alike. When *like* or *as* is used to compare two things, the comparison is called a **simile**. A **metaphor** makes a comparison by speaking of one thing as if it were another.

Sometimes a writer will give human characteristics to nonhuman things. Objects, ideas, places, or animals may be given human qualities. They may perform human actions. This kind of language is called **personification**.

Examples: *His feet* smelled <u>like</u> *dead fish*. (simile)
               Paul Bunyan was as big <u>as</u> a *tree*. (simile)
               The deep *lake* was a *golden mirror* reflecting the setting sun. (metaphor)
               The *old tree moaned with pain* in the cold wind. (personification)

The sentences below include figurative language. Rewrite each sentence. Express the same idea without using figurative language.

1. I was as jumpy as a cat in a roomful of rocking chairs.

   _____

2. As I looked out over the audience, my heart was a brick in my chest.

   _____

3. I touched the piano keys, and my fingers were like fence posts.

   _____

4. Luckily for me, the performance was as smooth as silk.

   _____

5. The last notes whispered, "You did just fine!"

   _____

Complete each sentence below by using figurative language.

6. The deserted old house was as dark as _____.

7. When I opened the squeaky front door, it creaked _____.

Name _____ Date _____

Remember that writers often use figurative language to compare unlike things. Figurative language uses figures of speech such as similes, metaphors, and personification. Figurative language gives a meaning that is not exactly that of the words used.

Read the paragraph below. Notice how the author uses figurative language to help you visualize the events and descriptions. Then, answer the questions.

Riding as fast as the wind, Sir Garland spurred his horse toward the castle. When he dashed across the open field, his shadow rode beside him like a good friend. When he galloped through the forest, the leaves whispered, "Hurry! Hurry!" The branches were enemies that caught at his sleeves. Sir Garland rounded a bend, and there before him was the castle, its glistening walls shining more brightly than the sun. "I must see the king!" Sir Garland shouted to the guards. "I bring the most important news in all the world!"

1. What comparison shows how fast Sir Garland was riding?

_____

2. What human characteristic did the author give to the leaves?

_____

3. What simile describes Sir Garland's shadow?

_____

4. What metaphor describes the branches?

_____

Write three sentences using figurative language.

5. _____

6. _____

7. _____

Idioms, Proverbs, and Adages

Idioms, proverbs, and adages are ways of making language more exciting by using words that bring strong images to mind.

An **idiom** is an expression that has a different meaning than that of the individual words in it.

Example: *Bob has a chip on his shoulder* means that Bob is upset about something that happened in the past. He does not actually have a chip on his shoulder.

A **proverb** is an old, familiar saying that often gives advice.

Example: *An apple a day keeps the doctor away* means that by eating healthful foods daily, you can avoid being sick.

An **adage** is a short saying that is frequently quoted and believed to be true.

Example: *No risk, no gain* means that if you expect to gain something, you have to be willing to risk something first.

Tell what each idiom, proverb, or adage means in your own words.

1. Good things come in small packages. _____

2. A leopard cannot change its spots. _____

3. He received a slap on the wrist for running the red light. _____

4. My mom says I am a backseat driver. _____

5. Don't count your chickens before they hatch. _____

6. Haste makes waste. _____

7. The coach had a knee-jerk reaction to hearing that I would be late to practice.

_____

8. When asked why the bill had not passed, the president tried to pass the buck to Congress.

_____

9. It was raining cats and dogs last night. _____

10. Variety is the spice of life. _____

11. I'm on the fence about going to the rodeo this weekend. _____

12. When it rains, it pours. _____

13. She was on pins and needles waiting for her exam results. _____

Dialect

Dialect refers to the way that people living in a particular region speak. Authors may have characters speak in dialect to make a story sound more realistic. Dialect uses its own words, grammar, and pronunciation that may be quite different from formal language.

Example: The cashier greeted us as we walked into the store. "How y'all doin'?" (dialect)
The cashier greeted us as we walked into the store. "How are you doing?" (formal)

Read the passage below and then rewrite the dialect using formal language.

"The boss jest called me into his office, an' told me they wouldn't need my services no more, an' paid me what was owin' me, an' that was jest $10. I tried to talk, but he kep' on writin' in a book an' didn't seem to hear me... The worst of it is, Minty, I dunno how we're going to live, or where I'll get work. It's mighty dull times now. It's a mean kind of a box I've got you into."

"Now, don't you go to talkin' like that, David May! I don't want to hear it. Git up an' wash you now, and eat your supper; the biscuits are all gettin' cold."

The poor fellow got up, threw his arms around his wife's waist, and leaned his head on his wife's shoulder...

"Well, mebbe we can weather it. I guess I can find some work pretty soon, an' you'll have enough to eat and wear. I guess we shall git along."

"I'd laugh if we couldn't."

From "A Wayfaring Couple" by Mary Eleanor Wilkins Freeman

_____

_____

_____

_____

_____

_____

_____

_____

_____

Name _____ Date _____

Paragraphs

A **paragraph** is a group of sentences that tells about one main idea. The first line of a paragraph is indented. This means the first word is moved in a little from the left margin.

The **topic sentence** expresses the main idea of the paragraph. It tells what all the other sentences in the paragraph are about. The topic sentence is often the first sentence in a paragraph.

The other sentences in a paragraph are **detail sentences**. Detail sentences add information about the topic sentence. They help the audience understand more about the main idea.

Example: Optical illusions occur when your eyes and brain give you the wrong idea about the way something looks. In one kind of optical illusion, the brain compares the images you see to images in your memory. Then, your brain makes the wrong interpretation about the new image. Another optical illusion takes place when the brain cannot choose between equally possible interpretations. In yet another, the brain works perfectly well. However, the bending of light through the atmosphere creates mirages that fool your eyes.

How to Write a Paragraph

1. Write a topic sentence that clearly tells the main idea of your paragraph.

2. Indent the first line.

3. Write detail sentences that tell about the main idea.

Complete this chart with details from the example paragraph.

Main Idea: _____

Detail: _____

Detail: _____

Detail: _____

Keeping to the Topic

Good writers keep to the point when they give information. Good writers make sure that each paragraph has a topic sentence and that every other sentence in the paragraph is about the topic sentence. Good writers plan a paragraph so that it gives details about one main idea.

Circle the letter of the sentence that keeps to the topic in the numbered sentence.

1. Indira Gandhi was an important leader in India during this century.

    a. John Kennedy was an important leader in the United States.

    b. In 1980, she was elected prime minister of India for the third time.

2. Indira Gandhi believed strongly in women's rights.

    a. She once said, "If a woman has the qualifications and ability for any profession, she should be in it."

    b. Her second son, Sanjay, was born in 1946.

3. When Indira was 12 years old, she organized other children in the "Monkey Brigade."

    a. Indira's father was Jawaharlal Nehru.

    b. The Monkey Brigade was very helpful to the Congress.

4. The Monkey Brigade took over many kinds of tasks from the Congress.

    a. They became good at cooking and serving food, making flags, and stuffing envelopes.

    b. Indira Gandhi lived for almost 67 years.

Draw a line through any sentences that are not about the topic sentence (the first sentence in the paragraph).

India's famous "March to the Sea" or "Salt March" was led by Mohandas K. Gandhi. My mother went to India last year. At that time, the British did not allow Indians to make their own salt. Not only that, but they had to buy their salt from British merchants. Cinnamon and ginger come from India. To defy this unfair law, Gandhi marched 200 miles to the sea, picking up thousands of Indians along the way. The Ganges is a river in India. Once there, Gandhi took a handful of salt from the beach. From that day onward, people all over India began to gather salt themselves.

Connecting a Main Idea and Details

In an expository paragraph, good writers express the main idea in a well-focused topic sentence. They connect the details and examples in the paragraph to the topic sentence and to each other.

These four sentences can be arranged as a paragraph. Write *M* for main idea or *D* for detail to identify each sentence.

_____ **1.** September 7 is Brazil's Independence Day.

_____ **2.** This holiday celebrates Brazil's independence from Portugal.

_____ **3.** The green and yellow colors of Brazil's flag are everywhere.

_____ **4.** People wear green and yellow T-shirts.

Read the sentences. Use the graphic organizer to arrange the main idea and details.

Other products of these new factories include shoes, textiles, construction equipment, and leather products. Some of these manufacturing plants produce cars, trucks, and farm equipment. Many large factories have been built in southern Brazil. Many of the goods produced in the factories of southern Brazil are shipped to the United States.

MAIN IDEA

_____
_____
_____

DETAIL

_____
_____
_____

DETAIL

_____
_____
_____

DETAIL

_____
_____
_____

Using Details to Explain

Good writers include details that give causes and effects. They tell their feelings in response to certain causes.

He was already an expert rider.
The Crow Indians had stolen some Sioux horses.
Slow had jabbed the Crow with his stick.
He no longer seemed so slow and serious.
He had a slow and serious nature.
It was considered braver to push an enemy
    off a horse than to shoot an arrow from far away.
Slow had acted bravely.
They had won the battle.

The numbered sentences tell about events. After each numbered sentence, write the detail sentence from the box that helps explain that event.

1. When Sitting Bull was a child, he was named Slow. _____

_____

2. At the age of ten, Slow was given his own pony. _____

_____

3. When Slow was fourteen, he and other Sioux fought some Crow Indians. _____

_____

4. Slow was armed only with a stick. _____

_____

5. One Crow Indian fell from his horse. _____

_____

6. The Sioux held a victory party. _____

_____

Narrative

A **narrative** is a story. It tells about real or made-up events. A narrative tells about one main idea. A narrative should have a beginning, a middle, and an end.

Most narratives have **dialogue**. A writer uses dialogue to show how characters speak to one another.

Example:

A Gleam in the Dust

Marc Haynes sadly waved good-bye to his friend Thomas and began to walk home. As he was walking, he saw something gleaming in the dirt. He bent over and picked up a coin. Then he read the date, and his eyes opened wide. The date on the coin was 1789!

Marc took the coin to Mr. Ortiz at the coin shop. "Well, Marc," Mr. Ortiz said, "this is a rare coin you've found. It was stolen from a private collection. I know that the owner is offering a reward of fifty dollars for the return of this coin."

Marc ran all the way home. "Wow!" he thought to himself. "I don't even have to leave town like Thomas did to have an adventure!"

How to Write a Story and Dialogue

1. Write an interesting beginning to present the main character and the setting.

2. Tell about a problem that the main character has to solve in the middle. Tell about what happens in order.

3. Write an ending. Tell how the main character solves the problem or meets the challenge.

4. Write a title for your story.

5. Place quotation marks before and after a speaker's exact words.

6. Use a comma to separate a quotation from the rest of the sentence unless a question mark or exclamation point is needed.

7. Begin a new paragraph each time the speaker changes.

8. Be sure the conversation sounds like real people talking. Use words that tell exactly how the character speaks.

Read the example narrative at the top of page 95. Then, answer the questions.

1. What is the problem in the narrative?

   _____

   _____

2. How is the problem solved?

   _____

   _____

3. Which two characters have dialogue?

   _____

   _____

Think about a story that you would like to tell. Use the graphic organizer to plan your narrative.

WRITING PLAN

Beginning	Middle	End
Characters:	Problem:	Solution:
Setting:		

96

Tips for Writing a Narrative
- Think about an exciting story to tell your reader.
- Create a realistic setting and at least three characters.
- Organize your ideas into a beginning, a middle, and an end.
- Write an interesting introduction that "grabs" your readers.
- Write a believable ending for your story.

Think about a story you would like to tell the readers. Use your writing plan as a guide for writing your narrative.

_____

_____

_____

_____

_____

_____

_____

_____

_____

_____

_____

_____

_____

_____

_____

_____

_____

_____

_____

To help your reader understand the sequence of events in your narrative, use **transitional words and phrases**. You can use words like *first, next,* and *finally* to show the time order of events. You can also use phrases like *at first, meanwhile,* and *at the end of the day* to connect parts of the narrative.

Examples: *First,* Joanne heard her alarm clock. *Next,* her cat jumped onto the bed. *Finally,* she got dressed and fed the cat.

                At first, I was afraid to start the steep climb. I put one foot hesitantly in front of the other. *Meanwhile,* my friends had started the climb behind me. They called out their encouragement. *At the end of the day,* we were all glad we had had this adventure together.

Use the words and phrases in the box or words of your own to create transitions between the sentences.

afterward	gradually	one morning
in the first place	suddenly	at first
the next day	once upon a time	initially
then	besides that	instead
as soon as	just before	but then

_____ there was a princess in a faraway land.

_____ she woke to find herself transformed into a frog.

_____ she was upset, _____ she found that

she liked being able to leap long distances. _____ she didn't miss having to

do homework every night. _____ she found a whole new circle of friends.

Write your own short narrative. Use transitions to link your ideas together.

_____

_____

_____

_____

_____

_____

_____

Including specific words and phrases, especially ones that relate to the five senses, helps give the reader the feeling of being inside the narrative.

Examples: When Liz stepped from the *cold* street into her grandmother's house, the *heat surrounded her like a warm blanket*. She *stamped* the snow from her boots and *rubbed her hands together briskly*. Grandma handed her a *steaming* cup of *hot chocolate* and led her to a *soft seat* by the *fire*. Her *woolly* poodle, Mortimer, *gently licked* Liz's hand, turned around *three* times, and lay *quietly* at her feet. Liz *sipped* from the *large blue mug*. It *tasted like home*.

Add words describing sight, sound, smell, hearing, or touch to the sentences below.

Lew found a diary belonging to his great-grandfather. The diary looked like

_____. The pages smelled like _____.

The cover felt like _____. As Lew flipped the pages,

he heard _____. When he closed his eyes, he could see

_____.

Write your own short narrative. Use words that will make readers feel as though they are experiencing the action. Try to appeal to the senses of sight, smell, taste, hearing, and touch.

_____

_____

_____

_____

_____

_____

_____

_____

_____

_____

Name _____ Date _____

Descriptive Paragraph

In a **descriptive paragraph**, a writer describes a person, place, thing, or event.

A good description lets the reader see, feel, hear, and sometimes taste or smell what is being described.

Example: Thanksgiving has to be my favorite holiday. The delicious aromas of turkey roasting and pumpkin pies baking fill the house. The lovely autumn colors of orange, gold, red, and brown can be seen in the special flower arrangements for the table. The sound of children laughing as they play games outside mixes with the music being played inside. The sights, smells, and sounds are very important to me.

How to Write a Descriptive Paragraph

1. Write a topic sentence that clearly tells what the paragraph is about.

2. Add detail sentences that give exact information about your topic.

3. Use colorful and lively words to describe the topic. Make an exact picture for the reader with the words you choose.

Complete this paragraph. Add descriptive words that appeal to your senses. Then, in the ( ), tell to what sense each descriptive word appeals.

One _____ (_____) night

we went to Loch Ness to see Nessie. We all wore _____

(_____) sweaters and gloves because of the _____

(_____) air. The sun set beyond the Loch, dropping like an

_____ (_____) ball.

_____ (_____) chirps interrupted

the quiet. A _____ (_____) fog

settled around us and made our clothes seem _____

(_____). Before we knew it, the _____

(_____) sun had appeared, but we had not seen Nessie.

Read the example description at the top of page 100. Then, answer the questions.

1. What is the writer describing in the paragraph?

   _____

2. What is the topic sentence?

   _____

3. What are some words the writer uses that appeal to your senses?

   _____

   _____

   _____

Think about something that you would like to describe. It could be a thing, a person you know, or something that has happened to you. Write it in the circle. Then, write words on the lines that describe your topic. Use the graphic organizer to plan your descriptive paragraph.

WRITING PLAN

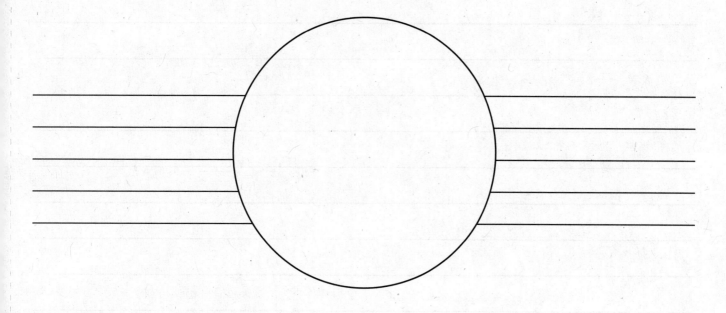

Tips for Writing a Descriptive Paragraph

- Describe a person, a place, an object, or an event.

- Paint a picture using words.

- Use words that appeal to the reader's senses. Let the reader see, smell, taste, feel, and hear what you are writing about.

- Include a sentence that introduces your topic.

- Write detail sentences that use descriptive words.

Think about something that you would like to describe. Introduce your topic in your first sentence. Then, use the words that you wrote in the graphic organizer on page 101 to describe it. Be sure to appeal to the reader's senses.

_____

_____

_____

_____

_____

_____

_____

_____

_____

_____

_____

_____

_____

_____

_____

How-to Paragraph

A **how-to paragraph** gives directions or explains how to do something.

Detail sentences in a how-to paragraph use time-order words to show the correct order of the steps.

Example:

Popping Popcorn in a Microwave Oven

Before you begin, be sure that you have popcorn that is especially packaged for microwave popping. Of course, you will need a microwave oven. Remove the plastic overwrap from the bag, and place it in the center of the microwave. Be very careful not to puncture or open the special bag the popcorn is in. You should set the microwave for full or 100-percent power. Then, set the timer for five minutes, and push the button to start. Stop the microwave when popping time slows to two to three seconds between pops. Remove the hot bag from the oven. You should shake the bag before opening it to increase flavor and to distribute the salt.

How to Write a How-to Paragraph

1. Write a topic sentence that names the process you are describing.

2. Add a detail sentence that tells what materials are needed.

3. Write detail sentences that tell the steps in the order they need to be done.

4. Use time-order words such as *first*, *next*, *then*, and *finally* to show the order of the steps.

Read the example how-to paragraph on page 103. Then, answer the questions.

1. What does this paragraph tell you how to do?

   _____

2. How many items are listed as materials, and what are they?

   _____

3. What is the first thing you must do?

   _____

4. What is the next thing you do?

   _____

5. What happens next?

   _____

6. What do you do last?

   _____

Think about something you want to tell others how to do. Use this writing plan to help you.

WRITING PLAN

1. What will you tell others how to do?

2. What materials are needed?

3. What steps must the reader follow? Number the steps.

4. What time-order words will you use?

Tips for Writing a How-to Paragraph

- Choose one thing to teach someone.
- Think of all the materials that are needed.
- Think of all the steps someone should follow.
- Be sure to write about the steps in the order they must be done.
- Use time-order words to help the reader follow the steps.
- Tell the reader any additional tips that will make the process easier to do.

Think about something you want to tell others how to do. Use your writing plan as a guide for writing your how-to paragraph.

_____

_____

_____

_____

_____

_____

_____

_____

_____

_____

_____

_____

_____

_____

_____

_____

_____

Informative Paragraph

An **informative paragraph** gives facts about one topic.

It has a topic sentence that tells the main idea. Detail sentences give facts about the main idea. Details can also include definitions, quotations, or other examples related to the topic. If you use a quotation, be sure to give its source.

Examples:

Food in Cans ⎤—— **title**

The idea of storing food in tin cans was developed in ⎤— **topic sentence**
England in 1810. A British merchant named Peter Durand is
responsible for this idea. It is interesting that no one invented
a can opener until sixty years later. British soldiers in 1812 tore **– detail sentences**
open canned rations with bayonets (long knives at the ends of **– definition**
rifles) and pocket knives. They were even known to shoot the
cans open.

The Modern Can Opener ⊢ **title**

The can opener that we use today was invented about ⎤— **topic sentence**
1870. It was invented by an American inventor named
William W. Lyman. It has a cutting wheel that rotates
around the can's edge. It was immediately popular, and it has
been changed only once. In 1925, a special wheel was added. **– detail sentences**
This was called the "feed wheel," and it made the can rotate
against the cutting wheel. Feed wheels are also used in other **– example**
kinds of tools and machinery.

How to Write an Informative Paragraph

1. Write a topic sentence that tells your main idea.

2. Write at least three detail sentences that give information about your main idea. Include definitions, quotations, and other examples related to the topic.

3. Think of a title for your informative paragraph.

Name _____ Date _____

Read the example informative paragraphs on page 106. Then, answer the questions.

1. What is the main idea of the first informative paragraph?

_____

_____

2. What are two supporting details in the first informative paragraph?

_____

_____

3. What is the topic sentence of the second informative paragraph?

_____

_____

4. What are two supporting details in the second informative paragraph?

_____

_____

Think about an informative topic you would like to write about. Use this writing plan to help you.

WRITING PLAN

Topic: _____

↓

Main idea:

↓   ↓   ↓

Detail 1:   Detail 2:   Detail 3:

Unit 5

Core Skills Language Arts, Grade 5

> **Tips for Writing an Informative Paragraph**
> - Choose one topic to write about.
> - Write a title for your paragraph.
> - Write a topic sentence that tells your main idea.
> - Write at least three detail sentences that tell facts about the main idea.
> - Be sure your facts are correct and complete.

Choose a topic you would like to write about. Use your writing plan as a guide for writing your informative paragraph.

_____

_____

_____

_____

_____

_____

_____

_____

_____

_____

_____

_____

_____

_____

_____

_____

_____

Compare and Contrast Paragraph

In a **compare and contrast paragraph**, a writer shows how two people, places, things, or ideas are alike or different. To compare means to show how two things are similar. To contrast means to show how two things are different. A writer may use words or phrases such as *especially, however, on the other hand,* and *in contrast* to link two different ideas. This helps highlight the differences between them.

Example: The Tasady tribe and the Ik tribe are two examples of people still living in the Stone Age. Neither tribe knew anything about the outside world until recently. The Tasady live in the mountain caves of the Philippine rain forests. In contrast, the Ik live in the mountains of Uganda, and they build grass huts for shelter. There is plenty of food in the Philippine rain forests, so the Tasady are comfortable and fairly well off. The Ik, however, face a constant lack of food. Ik usually eat any food they find right away. The Tasady have an especially good chance of surviving; the Ik, on the other hand, face an uncertain future.

How to Write a Compare and Contrast Paragraph

1. Write a topic sentence that names the subjects and tells briefly how they are alike and different.

2. Give examples in the detail sentences that clearly tell how the subjects are alike and different.

3. Write about the likenesses or differences in the same order you named them in the topic sentence. Use words and phrases such as *especially, however, on the other hand,* and *in contrast* to link ideas.

4. Try to have at least three ways in which the subjects are alike or different.

Name _____ Date _____

Read the example compare and contrast paragraph on page 109. Then, answer the questions.

1. What is the topic sentence of the paragraph? _____

_____

2. What two subjects are being compared? _____

_____

3. What are three things that are similar about the two subjects?

_____

_____

4. What are three things that are different about the two subjects?

_____

_____

5. Does the last sentence of the paragraph compare or contrast the survival of the tribes?

_____

Choose two things you want to write about. Write them on the lines below. Then, use the Venn diagram to help you plan your writing. List what is true only about A in the A circle. List what is true only about B in the B circle. List what is true about both A and B where the circles overlap.

A _____   B _____

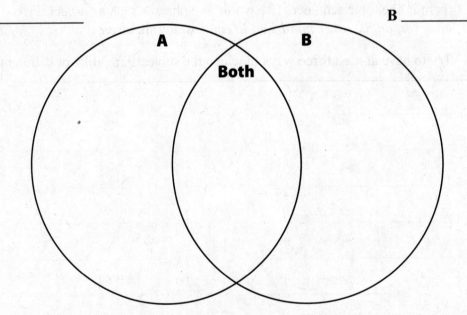

Tips for Writing a Compare and Contrast Paragraph

- Think about your two subjects.
- Decide how the two subjects are alike and different. Choose at least three important similarities and differences.
- Write a topic sentence that tells how the two subjects are alike and different.
- Explain how the two subjects are alike.
- Explain how the two subjects are different.
- Write about the likenesses or differences in the same order you named them in the topic sentence.

Choose two subjects you would like to compare and contrast. Use your Venn diagram to write your compare and contrast paragraph.

_____

_____

_____

_____

_____

_____

_____

_____

_____

_____

_____

_____

_____

_____

_____

Cause and Effect Paragraph

A cause is an event that makes something else happen. An effect is something that happens as a result of a cause. One cause may have several effects. One effect may have several causes.

In a **cause and effect paragraph**, a writer focuses on a cause that results in certain effects or an effect that can be traced back to its causes. This type of paragraph can begin with either the cause or the effect. A writer uses words or phrases such as *however, first of all, as a result,* and *furthermore* to link ideas. In a cause and effect paragraph, these words can help show a sequence of events.

Example: In the story "The Tournament," a girl named Katharine goes back in time. If Merlin had not reversed Katharine's wish in the story, however, history would have been very different. First of all, Katharine would have been the champion of the jousting tournament instead of Sir Launcelot. As a result, Sir Launcelot would have been dismissed from the Queen's order of knights. Furthermore, King Arthur's Round Table would have been dissolved and never heard of again.

How to Write a Cause and Effect Paragraph

1. Begin paragraphs of effect with a cause. Write a topic sentence that tells what happened. The detail sentences should all discuss effects.

2. Begin paragraphs of cause with an effect. Write a topic sentence that tells a result. The detail sentences should all discuss causes.

3. Write detail sentences in the order in which the effects or the causes happened. Use words or phrases such as *however, first of all, as a result,* and *furthermore* to help show a sequence of events.

Name _____ Date _____

Read the example cause and effect paragraph on page 112. Then, answer the questions.

1. What caused history to be in danger of change?

_____

_____

2. What caused history not to be changed?

_____

_____

3. What would be three effects if history had been changed?

_____

_____

_____

_____

Think of something that happened. What caused it to happen? What were the effects? Use the chart to organize your ideas.

WRITING PLAN

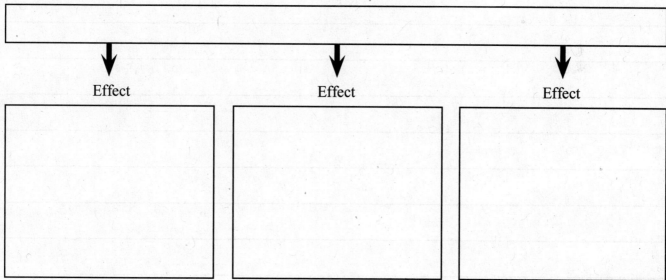

Cause

Effect   Effect   Effect

Tips for Writing a Cause and Effect Paragraph

- Think of something that happened.
- In your topic sentence, identify a cause or an effect.
- Clearly explain the cause that made something happen.
- Clearly explain the effect that happened because of something else.
- Try to include an end result or effect.

Choose an event you would like to write about. Use your writing plan as a guide for writing your cause and effect paragraph.

_____

_____

_____

_____

_____

_____

_____

_____

_____

_____

_____

_____

_____

_____

_____

_____

Evaluation Paragraph

In an **evaluation paragraph**, a writer judges a subject or an idea. Then, the writer provides reasons or examples to support this judgment. A writer might like or dislike something. A writer might also judge that something is good or bad.

Example: In the story "Two of Everything," Mr. and Mrs. Hak-Tak made doubles of themselves. They were very clever to make their doubles their neighbors. First, the Hak-Taks could not send their doubles away without telling the secret. Keeping them was a clever way of protecting themselves. Second, building a house next door for their doubles gave Mr. and Mrs. Hak-Tak extra help around the farm. Most important, their doubles became Mr. and Mrs. Hak-Tak's best friends. This was the cleverest outcome of all.

How to Write an Evaluation Paragraph

1. In the topic sentence, state whom or what you will evaluate and your judgment about it.

2. Keep your audience in mind as you write.

3. Provide reasons or strong examples to support your judgment.

4. Write a concluding sentence that summarizes your judgment.

Read the judgment and the three supporting reasons. Write *1* next to the most important reason, *2* next to the second most important reason, and *3* next to the least important reason.

Athletic contests between schools are a bad idea.

_____ Such contests lead to bad feelings between schools, and sometimes violent behavior is the result.

_____ It is too expensive to transport students from one place to another.

_____ Athletes spend too much time practicing, and their schoolwork suffers.

Name _____ Date _____

Read the example evaluation paragraph on page 115. Then, answer the questions.

1. What is being evaluated in the paragraph?

   _____

2. What judgment does the writer make about the Hak-Taks creating doubles?

   _____

3. What is the least important example the writer gives to support the judgment?

   _____

4. What is the second most important example the writer gives to support the judgment?

   _____

   _____

5. What is the most important example the writer gives to support the judgment?

   _____

   _____

Think of a subject or an idea that you would like to evaluate. Then, use this writing plan to organize your evaluation paragraph.

WRITING PLAN

Topic Sentence: _____

_____

Example: _____

Example: _____

Example: _____

Tips for Writing an Evaluation Paragraph
- Choose one subject or idea to evaluate.
- Decide what your judgment will be.
- Identify your subject and your judgment in your topic sentence.
- Include at least three reasons or examples for your judgment.
- Put your least important reason first in your paragraph.
- Put your most important reason last in your paragraph.

Choose a subject or an idea you would like to evaluate. Use your writing plan as a guide for writing your evaluation paragraph.

_____

_____

_____

_____

_____

_____

_____

_____

_____

_____

_____

_____

_____

Opinion Paragraph

In an **opinion paragraph**, a writer tries to make readers agree with his or her opinion on an issue. The writer uses words and phrases such as *consequently, in addition, because,* and *specifically* to link his or her opinion with the supporting reasons.

Example:

	Wisconsin should have a "Caddie Woodlawn Day" to celebrate the trust between Caddie and her Native American friends. This trust prevented a massacre and led to the peace between the two groups. Specifically, "Caddie Woodlawn Day" would remind us to settle problems by peaceful means. In addition, this holiday would give us a reason to practice our ancestors' customs. Consequently, we would be reminded to appreciate their way of life. Because this holiday would help us to remember Caddie Woodlawn, the state legislature should vote in favor of this idea.	**opinion in topic sentence**
linking word		**reasons and facts**
		strongest reason last
linking word		**restated opinion or call for action**

How to Write an Opinion Paragraph

1. Write a topic sentence that states the issue and your opinion about it.

2. Keep in mind the audience that you want to convince.

3. Give at least three reasons that will convince your audience to agree with you. Include these reasons in the detail sentences. Use words and phrases such as *consequently, in addition, because,* and *specifically* to link your opinion with the supporting reasons.

4. Explain each reason with one or more examples.

5. Save your strongest reason for last.

6. At the end of your paragraph, tell your opinion again. Ask your reader to feel the same way.

Name _____ Date _____

Read the example opinion paragraph on page 118. Then, answer the questions.

1. What is the writer's main idea in this paragraph?

   _____

   _____

2. What are two reasons the writer gives to support the main idea?

   _____

   _____

   _____

3. What call for action does the writer have in the last sentence?

   _____

   _____

Think of something you feel strongly about. Then, use this writing plan to organize your opinion paragraph.

WRITING PLAN

My Opinion

↓

Reason	**Reason**	**Reason**

↓   ↓   ↓

Example	**Example**	**Example**

Tips for Writing an Opinion Paragraph

• Choose a topic that you feel strongly about.

• State your opinion in your topic sentence.

• Write good reasons to support your opinion.

• Try to have at least three good reasons.

• Save your strongest reason for last.

• Try to give an example for each reason.

• At the end of your paragraph, restate your opinion.

• Tell the reader to take some action.

Choose a topic that you have an opinion about. Use your writing plan as a guide for writing your opinion paragraph.

_____

_____

_____

_____

_____

_____

_____

_____

_____

_____

_____

_____

_____

_____

_____

_____

_____

_____

Using a Dictionary

Words in a dictionary are listed in **alphabetical order**—the order of letters from A to Z.

There are two **guide words** at the top of every dictionary page. The word on the left is the first word on the page. The word on the right is the last. All other words are in alphabetical order between the guide words.

Each word defined in the dictionary is an **entry word**. An entry word usually appears in dark print. It appears in alphabetical order and is divided into syllables.

An **entry** is all the information about an entry word.

A **definition** is the meaning of a word. Many words have more than one definition. Each definition is numbered.

The **part of speech** tells whether a word is a noun, a verb, or some other part of speech. The parts of speech in a dictionary entry usually are abbreviated this way:

noun—n.   verb—v.   adjective—adj.   adverb—adv.   pronoun—pron.

A definition is often followed by an **example** that shows how to use the word.

---

float [flōt] **1** *v.* To rest or cause to rest on the surface of a liquid, such as water, without sinking: A life preserver *floats*. **2** *n.* An object that floats or holds up something else in a liquid, as an anchored raft at a beach or a piece of cork attached to a fishing line. **3** *v.* To be carried along gently on the surface of a liquid or through the air; drift: Fog *floated* over the city. **4** *v.* To move lightly and without effort: The skater *floated* across the ice. **5** *n.* A wheeled platform or truck on which an exhibit is carried in a parade.

Use the example entry to answer the following questions.

1. How many definitions are given for *float*? _____

2. Which part of speech is the first definition of *float*? _____

3. As what other part of speech can *float* be used? _____

4. Which definition tells the meaning of *float* in each of the following sentences?

   The balloon <u>floated</u> up to the ceiling. _____

   Have you ever ridden a <u>float</u> in a parade? _____

A **syllable** is a word part that has only one vowel sound. Each entry word in the dictionary is divided into syllables.

A **pronunciation** follows each entry word. Letters and symbols show how the word is pronounced. It also shows the number of syllables in the word.

Example: **il • lu • sion** [i • loo′ zhen] *n.* **1** A false, mistaken idea or belief: to lose childish *illusions*. **2** A deceiving appearance or the false impression it gives: an optical *illusion*.

In a word with two or more syllables, the **accent mark** (′) in the pronunciation shows which syllable is said with the most force.

A **pronunciation key** explaining the pronunciation marks usually appears at the beginning of a dictionary.

a	add	i	it	o͞o	took	oi	oil
ā	ace	ī	ice	o͞o	pool	ou	pout
â	care	o	odd	u	up	ng	ring
ä	palm	ō	open	û	burn	th	thin
e	end	ô	order	yo͞o	fuse	th	this
ē	equal					zh	vision

ə = { a in *above*   e in *sicken*   i in *possible*
      { o in *melon*   u in *circus*

Write the word shown in each dictionary respelling. Then, use each word in a sentence. Use the dictionary if you need help with pronunciations or definitions.

1. [op′ ti • kəl] _____

_____

2. [ri • flek′ shən] _____

_____

3. [mə • jish′ ən] _____

_____

4. [nā′ chər] _____

_____

A dictionary is a good resource to use to check the spelling and meaning of words. Here are some tips for looking up a word when you do not know the correct spelling.

1. Make your best guess about the word's spelling based on how the word is pronounced. If you can figure out the first few letters of a word, finding the correct spelling should be fairly easy. Keep in mind that some sounds can be spelled in multiple ways. For example, the "f" sound can be spelled "ph."

2. Go to the letter of the alphabet that you think the word begins with. Use the guide words to help you locate the page for the word.

3. Scan down the list of entry words until you see the word.

4. Check the meaning to be sure you have found the right word.

Each sentence has one misspelled word. Look up the word in the dictionary and write the correct spelling.

1. Knocking the glass of water off the table was an <u>acident</u>. _____

2. I felt <u>despeir</u> about the test because I had not studied. _____

3. My dog barks loudly to <u>gaurd</u> our house from strangers. _____

4. Did you <u>reconize</u> the actor when he came to our class? _____

5. If Dad sits on his hat, he will <u>sqash</u> it. _____

6. I laughed <u>througout</u> the comedian's performance. _____

7. Our family reserved a campground for its <u>anual</u> reunion. _____

8. When I started playing the violin, I found it very <u>diffcult</u>. _____

9. I love <u>histery</u> class because there are so many interesting people to read about. _____

10. My little sister was <u>talketive</u> after sleeping all afternoon. _____

Using a Thesaurus

A **thesaurus** is a book that tells synonyms, words that have nearly the same meaning, and antonyms, words that mean the opposite of a word. Many thesauruses are like dictionaries. The entry words are listed in dark print in alphabetical order. Guide words at the top of the page tell which words can be found on the page. Good writers use a thesaurus to find vivid and exact words to make their writing more interesting.

Replace each underlined word or words with words that express the meaning in a more exact and vivid way. You may want to refer to a thesaurus.

1. When Harvey was growing up, his family was <u>very large</u>. _____

2. At one time Harvey counted <u>about</u> sixty cousins. _____

3. They all lived on a large farm, <u>taking care of</u> animals and crops. _____

4. Everyone <u>worked hard</u>. _____

5. In the 1930s, the family lost the land they had <u>worked</u> for so long. _____

6. Things became very <u>hard</u> for the family. _____

7. Harvey's parents found jobs in the <u>shops</u> in town. _____

8. Harvey, an <u>ambitious</u> young man, decided that he would have his own store someday.

_____

9. Thirty years later, Harvey owned one of the largest chains of stores in the <u>country</u>.

_____

Write sentences using exact, vivid synonyms of the words in parentheses.

10. (small) _____

_____

11. (house) _____

_____

12. (walk) _____

_____

Parts of a Book

The **title page** tells the name of a book and the name of the author. It also gives the name of the publisher and the city of publication.

The **copyright page** tells when the book was published. It sometimes lists the titles of other books from which material was reprinted by permission. This is the acknowledgments section.

The **table of contents** comes after the title page. It lists each unit, chapter, story, or section in the order in which it appears in the book. A table of contents usually lists the page on which each part of the book begins.

Many nonfiction books also have an **index**. An index is an alphabetical list of all the topics in a book. Indexes include the page or pages on which each topic appears.

Giants *in Myth and Legend* by Gloria Kim KING PRESS, INC. New York Chicago	Copyright © 1983 by King Press, Inc. **Acknowledgments** Ace Publishing Company: from *Giants* by Val Meyer. Copyright © 1981 by Val Meyer. All rights reserved. Printed in the United States of America.	**CONTENTS** The Greek Titans......................1 The Greek Cyclopes ....17 Jack and the Beanstalk...........21 Jack the Giant-Killer..............35 The Iroquois Stone Giants .....45 Paul Bunyan..........................51 Glossary ....65 Index 73
Title Page	**Copyright Page**	**Table of Contents**

Use the example pages to answer the following questions.

1. What is the title of this book? _____

2. Which company published the book? _____

3. When and where was the book printed? _____

4. How many chapters are there? _____

5. How many chapters tell of giants that are Greek? _____

6. On what page could you begin to read about Paul Bunyan? _____

7. On what page does the index begin? _____

8. Which is the first page on which you might read about Polyphemus, one of the Cyclopes?

_____

Reading for Information

Skimming is a quick reading method. To skim is to look at material in order to note its general subject, its divisions, and its major headings.

Scanning is also a quick reading method. To scan is to look quickly at a particular passage, searching for key words.

Skim the table of contents of this book to answer questions 1–3. Scan the paragraph from the book to answer questions 4–6.

Bring in all objects that are usually left outside, such as lawn furniture or garbage cans. If you cannot bring them inside, tie them down securely. Board up your windows so that they will not be broken by objects carried by the wind. When the hurricane hits, stay inside and listen to your radio for information. Do not go outside until the authorities announce that it is safe.

1. How many general subjects will this book cover? _____

   What are they? _____

2. What does Chapter 1 of each part explain? _____

3. What do Chapters 2 and 3 of each part explain? _____

   _____

4. What should you do with lawn furniture if you cannot bring it inside?

   _____

5. Why should you board up your windows? _____

   _____

6. When can you go outside again? _____

   _____

Taking Notes

Good writers take notes to remember the facts they find when doing research for a report.

It is often helpful to write notes on cards. When preparing to write a report, the writer can put the cards in order according to the topic.

Example: The Mythological Zoo by Elizabeth Dixon, pages 20–29
Which Greek and Roman gods had "pet" birds?
Zeus: eagle
Hera: peacock
Apollo: crow

How to Take Notes

1. Record the name of the book or magazine from which you are taking the information.

2. List the main topic of the material.

3. Write the most important facts and details.

4. Use key words and phrases. You need not write complete sentences.

5. Be sure your notes are accurate and readable.

Read this information taken from page 21 of <u>The Mythological Zoo</u>. Write notes that answer the question "What are the symbols of Zeus?"

The Greeks and Romans both had many gods. However, each of these ancient peoples had one god whom they considered to be the most important. Jupiter was considered the king of the Roman gods. Zeus held the same position for the Greeks. Jupiter's symbols were the king's scepter and the thunderbolt. Zeus was known by these two symbols, as well as by the oak tree and the eagle.

_____

_____

_____

_____

_____

_____

When taking notes, remember to write down the name of your source. You should also write down the most important information in the source. Take notes only on the material you will use in your essay or report.

Read the following paragraph. As you read, take notes on the lines below. Remember to focus on key points and to use abbreviations.

One of the hottest and driest places in North America is Death Valley, in California. An average of only about one and one half inches of rain falls each year in Death Valley, and in some years it does not rain at all. The valley is the bottom of a lake that dried up in prehistoric times, leaving clay and salt in the center of the valley and sand dunes to the north. Near Badwater is the lowest spot in North America. It is 282 feet below sea level!

My Notes _____

_____

_____

_____

_____

Now read over the notes you took. Use your notes to answer the questions.

1. How did you choose the points to include in your notes?

_____

2. What abbreviations did you use in your notes?

_____

3. Why is it important to take good notes?

_____

128

Using Quotations

Good writers use **quotations** from oral and written sources. Quotations are the exact words that are in a book or that a speaker says. Quotations are enclosed in quotation marks (" ").

Each numbered sentence below is the topic sentence of a paragraph in a research report about whales. The box contains sentences with quotations that might be used in the report. Before each topic sentence, write the letter of the quotation sentence that should be included in that paragraph.

a. "These magnificent creatures are even larger than the famous dinosaurs that died out so long ago," commented Dr. Romley.

b. Said Dr. Schultz, "Although international laws ban hunting, some species of whales are still in danger of extinction."

c. Mr. Walters explained, "The whale's nostrils, located on top of its head, can be tightly closed so that no water leaks in."

d. "I am still thrilled every time I hear these whales 'talking' to each other," said Mr. Clark.

e. "Though we often think of whales as huge animals," said Ms. Kwong, "some species are barely four feet long."

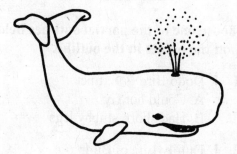

f. "A baleen whale has no teeth. Instead, it has thin plates, called baleen, in its mouth," added Mr. Walters.

_____ **1.** A whale's body is specially adapted for its underwater life.

_____ **2.** Whales vary greatly in size.

_____ **3.** The blue whale is the largest animal that ever lived.

_____ **4.** Whales make special sounds to communicate with each other and to navigate through the water.

_____ **5.** Some species of whales have become endangered animals.

_____ **6.** Baleen whales form one of the two major groups of whales.

Rough Draft

A writer quickly puts all of his or her ideas on paper in a **rough draft**.

How to Write a Rough Draft

1. Read your outline and notes. Keep them near you as you write.

2. Follow your outline to write a rough draft. Do not add anything that is not on your outline. Do not leave out anything.

3. Write one paragraph for each Roman numeral in your outline.

4. Write freely. Do not worry about mistakes now. You will revise later.

5. Read over your rough draft. Make notes on changes you want to make.

Choose one of the partial outlines below. Then, write a topic sentence and two detail sentences based upon the points in the outline.

1. I. Dodo Bird Is Extinct
   A. Could not fly
   B. Had short, stubby legs

2. I. Family Life of Birds
   A. Selecting a territory
   B. Building a nest

3. I. Bird Migration
   A. Why birds migrate
   B. Where birds migrate

Topic sentence: _____

_____

Detail sentence 1: _____

_____

Detail sentence 2: _____

_____

Analyzing a Research Report

A **research report** gives information about a topic. It draws facts from various sources. It has a title, an introduction, a body, and a conclusion.

Read the research report. Answer the questions that follow.

Many of our superstitions came to us from very ancient sources. The idea that one should knock on wood for good luck, for example, is a 4,000-year-old custom that began with some Native American tribes of North America. Noticing that the oak was struck often by lightning, members of the tribe thought that it must be the dwelling place of a sky god. They also thought that boasting of a future personal deed was bad luck and meant the thing would never happen. Knocking on an oak tree was a way of contacting the sky god and being forgiven for boasting.

Another interesting superstition is that it is bad luck to open an umbrella indoors. In eighteenth-century England, umbrellas had stiff springs and very strong metal spokes. Opening one indoors could indeed cause an accident. It could injure someone or break a fragile object. This superstition came about for practical reasons.

1. What would be a good title for this research report?

   _____

2. What is the topic of the first paragraph?

   _____

3. What is the topic of the second paragraph?

   _____

4. What are three details from the first paragraph?

   _____

   _____

   _____

Research Report

After making the changes to the rough draft, the writer can complete the final copy of the research report.

Example:

Bird Myths and Mysteries

Birds have always been part of myths and legends. In ancient Greece, many birds were special to the gods. The eagle was a symbol of Zeus. The peacock symbolized Hera, and the crow stood for Apollo. Stories tell of bird-like monsters called Harpies and of a huge, terrible bird called a roe.

Birds are still used as symbols today. Many expressions compare people to birds. A person may be "wise as an owl" or "proud as a peacock." Names of birds can also be found in the world of politics. Senators are often described as hawks or doves, depending on their political point of view.

Scientists have solved some of the mysteries about birds, but many others remain. How do the ptarmigan's feathers act as a camouflage? Why does the arctic tern migrate from the Arctic to the Antarctic? These and other mysteries are sure to keep people fascinated by birds.

How to Write a Research Report

1. Read over your rough draft. Add any material you might have forgotten.

2. Make all revising and editing changes.

3. Write the title of your report.

4. Write the report from your rough draft and your notes.

5. Indent the first sentence of each paragraph.

6. Complete your bibliography.

Read the example research report on this page. Then, choose a topic that interests you, and write your own report. Remember to take notes, make an outline, write a rough draft, complete a bibliography, and then write your report. Save all your notes to turn in with your report. Your report should be at least three paragraphs long and should have a title.

Answer Key

page 1
Descriptions of what nouns name may vary. **1.** sense, thing; smell, thing; nose, thing; **2.** people, person; smell, thing; food, thing; grass, thing; rain, thing; **3.** People, person; enjoyment, thing; odors, thing; **4.** eggs, thing; odor, thing; **5.** sense, thing; smell, thing; person, person; danger, idea; **6–7.** Sentences will vary.

page 2
1. common: scientist; proper: Maryland, **2.** common: friends; proper: Benjamin Banneker, **3.** common: People, accomplishments; proper: United States, **4.** proper: Banneker, Washington, D.C., **5.** common: man, memory, **6.** common: astronomer, nights, stars, planets, **7.** common: scientists, planets; proper: Mars, Jupiter, **8.** common: changes, country; proper: Banneker, **1–8.** Rewritten sentences will vary.

page 3
1. tornado, singular; hurricane, singular; **2.** minutes, plural; hours, plural; **3.** winds, plural; **4.** air, singular; fire, singular; **5.** conditions, plural; signs, plural; **6.** The girls ate their lunches on the school benches., **7.** The young ladies looked at the dark clouds overhead., **8.** Strong winds picked up boxes of books by the library doors.

page 4
1. trout, **2.** fish or fishes, **3.** heroes, **4.** women, **5.** men, **6.** mice, **7.** beliefs, **8.** wolves, **9.** oxen, **10.** calves, **11.** children, **12.** feet, **13.** lives

page 5
1. My friend's mother had a baby yesterday., **2.** The baby's teeth are not in yet., **3.** The child's head is still soft., **4.** The bib's tie is torn., **5.** The crib's sheets are pink., **6.** The uncle's smile is happy., **7.** The grandmother's gift is a new blanket., **8.** The father's pleasure is easy to see., **9.** The infant's eyes are blue., **10.** My friend's life will be different now.

page 6
1. Imagine the children's surprise!, **2.** They found the robins' baby on the sidewalk., **3.** They returned it to the parents' nest., **4.** They watched the adult birds' activities for a while., **5.** The animals' fear was apparent., **6.** The humans' odor was on the baby bird., **7.** The bird was now the young people's responsibility., **8.** The students' job was to find a shoe box., **9.** The parents' job was to find some soft lining.

page 7
1. They, Explorers; **2.** It, animal; **3.** them, animals or kangaroos; **4.** They, birds or emus and cassowaries; **5.** It, platypus; **6.** They, Scientists; **7.** It, coolabah or tree; **8.** It, flower or kangaroo paw; **9.** They, trees; **10.** they, trunks

page 8
1. We read about the Wrights last week., **2.** It was he who found the book., **3.** They grew up in Dayton, Ohio., **4.** He was a bishop there., **5.** She helped care for them., **6.** It was a gift from their father., **7.** He was four years older than Orville., **8.** On December 17, 1903, it took place., **9.** It lasted 12 seconds., **10.** They were 13 seconds, 15 seconds, and 59 seconds.

page 9
1. Darkness covered them., **2.** The game wardens noticed it., **3.** Then, the game wardens saw them., **4.** Two men and a woman were searching it for alligators., **5.** The game wardens pushed it out of the brush., **6.** They raced toward them., **7.** The powerful engine moved it quickly over the water., **8.** The poachers quickly dumped them back into the water., **9.** The wardens searched the inside of it.

page 10
1. He, subject pronoun; **2.** him, object pronoun; **3.** We, subject pronoun; **4.** them, object pronoun; **5.** She, subject pronoun; **6.** her, object pronoun; **7.** They, subject pronoun; **8.** them, object pronoun; **9.** She, subject pronoun; **10.** them, object pronoun

page 11
1. myself, **2.** himself, **3.** itself, **4.** herself, **5.** yourselves, **6.** ourselves, **7.** yourself, **8.** ourselves, **9.** herself, **10.** myself, **11.** herself, **12.** himself

page 12
1. their, before a noun; **2.** Its, before a noun; **3.** hers, stands alone; **4.** Her, before a noun; **5.** theirs, stands alone; **6.** our, before a noun; **7.** her; **8.** hers; **9.** their; **10.** your

page 13
1. He, Mr. Les Harsten; **2.** them, plants; **3.** He, Les; **4.** It, sound; **5.** it, plant; **6.** them, sounds; **7.** It, recording; **8.** They, plants; **9.** It, music; **10.** They, plants

page 14
1. spectacular, what kind; **2.** superb, what kind; beautiful, what kind; **3.** winter, what kind; **4.** twelve, how many; different, what kind; **5.** red, what kind; pink, what kind; violet, what kind; white, what kind; **6.** spongy, what kind; acid, what kind; **7.** three, how many; four, how many; flowering, what kind; **8.** Sweet, what kind; fragrant, what kind; special, what kind

page 15
1. Greek, Greece; **2.** Spartan, Sparta; **3.** Athenian, Athens; **4.** Roman, Rome; **5.** Korean, Korea; **6.** Romanian, Romania; **7.** English; **8.** Norwegian; **9.** Canadian; **10.** American

page 16
1. crunchy, peanuts; 2. salty, They; 3. red, skin; 4. delicious, seeds; 5. inedible, seeds; 6. popular, They; 7. healthful, snacks; 8. sour, apples; 9. crisp and juicy, fruit; 10. noisy, vegetable; 11–15. Adjectives will vary.

page 17
1. a, 2. These, 3. the, 4. this, 5. a, 6. the, 7. a, 8. this, 9. these, 10. those

page 18
1. more wonderful, 2. most beautiful, 3. highest, 4. deeper, 5. biggest, 6. largest, 7. easiest, 8. most unusual, 9. stranger, 10. more excited, 11. most interesting, 12. oldest

page 19
1. better, 2. less, 3. worst, 4. more, 5. worse, 6. more, 7. Many, 8. most, 9. better, 10. best

page 20
1. linking: felt, 2. action: left, 3. action: needed, 4. action: looked, 5. action: saw, 6. action: ran; action: studied, 7. linking: appeared, 8. action: pulled; action: moved, 9. action: slid, 10. action: hurried, 11. action: bowed, 12. linking: was

page 21
1. told, main verb; 2. looking, main verb; 3. tell, main verb; 4. was, helping verb; 5. leaned, main verb; 6. was, helping verb; 7. fallen, main verb; 8. was, helping verb

page 22
1. likes, 2. visits, 3. comes, 4. fix, 5. mixes, 6. takes, 7. show, 8. wishes, 9. worries, 10. watches, 11. makes, 12. needs

page 23
1. walked, 2. sampled, 3. seemed, 4. described, 5. served, 6. sipped, 7. fried, 8. tried, 9. passed, 10. pinned, 11. featured, 12. tasted

page 24
1. will happen, 2. will hunt, 3. will gather, 4. Will (Sam) miss, 5. Will (they) search, 6. will (not) find, 7. will remember, 8. will cook, 9. will float, 10. will hide, 11. will notice, 12. Will (Sam) leave

page 25
1. look, present; 2. have, present; 3. climbs, present; 4. make, present; 5. climbed, past; 6. jumped, past; 7. will see, future; 8. will go, future; 9. will ride, future; 10. will tell, future; 11. Sam will see ten lizards., 12. I will see only four., 13. Some lizards will change colors.

page 26
1. had spent, 2. has found, 3. will have taken, 4. had checked, 5. have read, 6. will have finished, 7. had started, 8. has walked, 9. will have gone, 10. had worried, 11. have studied

page 27
1. writes; Yesterday Talya wrote a sentence on the board., 2. beat; He usually beats all the other competitors at a swim meet., 3. will blow; The wind often blows leaves down our street., 4. goes; Ms. Martin went to Norway last year., 5–8. Sentences will vary but should use the same tense for all three verbs.

page 28
1. done, 2. rode, 3. gave, 4. ran, 5. come, 6. ate, 7. saw, 8. said, 9. took, 10. thought, 11. written, 12. went

page 29
1. began, 2. grew, 3. known, 4. chosen, 5. spoken, 6. flew, 7. worn, 8. lost, 9. found, 10. torn, 11. rang, 12. caught, 13. swum, 14. brought, 15. sang

page 30
1. her, 2. immigrants, 3. torch, 4. hope, freedom, 5. statue, 6–16. Sentences will vary. Be sure each sentence contains an appropriate direct object.

page 31
1. carefully, how; 2. First, when; 3. Next, when; 4. Then, when; 5. Finally, when; 6. firmly, how; 7. surely, how; 8. joyfully, how; 9. higher, where; 10. Soon, when; 11. down, where; 12–13. Sentences will vary. Be sure each sentence contains an adverb.

page 32
1. more eagerly, 2. more strongly, 3. most courageously, 4. more completely, 5. more often, 6. most convincingly, 7. better, 8. worse, 9. better, 10. well

page 33
1. very, 2. extremely, 3. carefully, 4. quite, 5. too, 6. fairly, 7. certainly, 8. rather, 9. much, 10. charming, 11. suggests, 12. uses, 13. (would) work, 14. decided, 15. less

page 34
1. gently, 2. great, 3. carefully, 4. completely, 5. firmly, 6. serious, 7. fairly, 8. entire, 9. good, 10. well, 11. well, 12. good

page 35
1. to her island, island; 2. below the waves, waves; 3. without any means, means; of navigation, navigation; except the stars, stars; 4. For many centuries, centuries; by the stars, stars; 5. in the 1700s, 1700s; 6. on the sea, sea; of celestial navigation, navigation; 7. of a star, star; 8. above the horizon, horizon; 9. from that reading, reading; 10. Without this information, information

page 36

1. in a car, in; 2. from the sea, from; 3. from the motion, from; of the waves, of; 4. In this same way, In; in the back, in; of a car, of; 5. of balance, of; 6. inside your ears, inside; 7. with a fluid, with; with special hairs, with; 8. of movement, of; 9. in the bottom, in; of the canals, of; 10. around the canals, around; 11. in your stomach, in; 12–14. Sentences will vary. Be sure that each sentence contains a prepositional phrase.

page 37

1. preposition, 2. adverb, 3. preposition, 4. adverb, 5. preposition, 6. adverb, 7. preposition, 8. preposition, 9. preposition, 10–13. Sentences will vary. Be sure that each sentence contains a prepositional phrase.

page 38

1. and, 2. but, 3. and, 4. or, 5. but, 6. or, 7. and, 8. and, 9. or, 10. and, 11. and, 12. but

page 39

1.-10. Answers will vary.

page 40

1. Gee!, 2. Wow!, 3. Oh, dear!, 4. Oh, my!, 5. Good grief!, 6. Oops!, 7. Great!, 8. Alas!, 9. Of course! 10–18. Interjections will vary.

page 41

1–9. Sentences will vary. Be sure each sentence contains a subject or predicate as needed.

page 42

1. We memorized the capitals of all of the states., 2. Everyone knew the capital of Arkansas., 3. The capital is not always the largest city in the state., 4. You should picture the map in your mind., 5. The left side is the west side., 6. not a sentence, 7. That river empties into the Gulf of Mexico., 8. not a sentence

page 43

1. predicate, 2. predicate, 3. subject, 4. subject, 5. predicate; 6. subject: The eye; predicate: is made of many parts., 7. subject: The pupil; predicate: is the round, black center of the eye., 8. subject: The outer, colored part; predicate: is called the iris., 9. subject: The iris; predicate: is made of a ring of muscle., 10. subject: Too much light; predicate: can damage the eye., 11. subject: The iris; predicate: closes up in bright light., 12. subject: Some people; predicate: are colorblind., 13. subject: They; predicate: cannot see shades of red and green., 14. subject: A nearsighted person; predicate: cannot see distant things well., 15. subject: Close objects; predicate: are blurry to a farsighted person; 16. subject: Farsighted people; predicate: often use reading glasses.

page 44

1. Two young men, men; 2. A raging tornado, tornado; 3. Two square miles of the city, miles; 4. An odd roaring noise, noise; 5. The strong wind, wind; 6. Giant walls, walls; 7. One side of a street, side; 8. The other side, side; 9. Some people, people; 10. A tornado, tornado; 11. This lucky person, person; 12. Unlucky people, people; 13. Dorothy, Dorothy; 14. She, She; 15. A ride in a tornado, ride

page 45

1. Sally and John; 2. Roses, daisies, and violets; 3. Jim and Meg, 4. Sally, John, Jim, and Meg; 5. basket and jug; 6. friends and dogs; 7. Apples, peaches, and plums; 8. Frankie and Joanne; 9. friends, dogs, and cats

page 46

1. can be very interesting, can be; 2. have found almost a million different types of insects, have found; 3. live almost everywhere on Earth's surface, live; 4. can study insects in the woods, streams, parks, and your own yard, can study; 5. has no backbone, has; 6. makes insects different from many animals, makes; 7. have six legs, have; 8. appeared about 400 million years ago, appeared; 9. live together in large groups, live; 10. capture insects and other small animals, capture; 11. use the insects for food, use; 12. attracts insects with its sweet nectar, attracts; 13. snaps its leaves shut on insects, snaps; 14. traps insects with a sticky liquid, traps

page 47

1. planned and prepared; 2. shopped, cleaned, and cooked; 3. hired and bought; 4. ordered and borrowed; 5. wore and played; 6. ate, laughed, and danced; 7. cleared and helped; 8. walked, ran, or rode; 9. sat and rested

page 48

1. subject: Our favorite coach, coach; predicate: cheers during the race, cheers; 2. subject: My youngest sister, sister; predicate: swims ahead of the others, swims; 3. subject: Her strokes, strokes; predicate: cut through the water, cut; 4. subject: Ripples, Ripples; predicate: splash at the edge of the pool, splash; 5. subject: The exciting race, race; predicate: ends with a surprise, ends; 6. subject: My sister's team, team; predicate: finishes first, finishes; 7. subject: The people in the bleachers, people; predicate: cheer wildly, cheer; 8. subject: The team, team; predicate: holds the silver trophy for a school photograph, holds; 9. subject: The team members, members; predicate: hug each other happily, hug

Answer Key
Core Skills Language Arts, Grade 5

page 49

1. subject: house, it; predicate: was, had; compound;
2. subject: Underground Railroad; predicate: brought;
simple; 3. subject: wagons; predicate: were; simple;
4. subject: rides; predicate: were; simple; 5. subject: slaves,
they; predicate: stopped, stayed; compound; 6. subject:
home; predicate: was; simple; 7. subject: Levi Coffin, he;
predicate: was, earned; compound; 8. subject: Dies Drear,
he; predicate: was, lived; compound; 9. subject: Allan
Pinkerton, he; predicate: made, hid; compound; 10. subject:
Harriet Tubman, she; predicate: led, took; compound

page 50

Sentence types may vary.

1. ., declarative; 2. ., declarative; 3. ?, interrogative; 4. !,
exclamatory; 5. ., imperative; 6. ., declarative; 7. ?,
interrogative; 8. !, exclamatory; 9. ., declarative; 10. .,
imperative, 11. ?, interrogative; 12. ., imperative

page 51

Students should circle sentence numbers 2, 3, 4, 6, and
7. 1. Trash, 2. (You), 3. (You), 4. (You), 5. problem,
6. (You), 7. (You), 8. Pieces, 9–12. Sentences may vary
slightly. 9. Avoid packages with too much wrapping.,
10. Buy the largest sizes of products., 11. Use old T-shirts
as wiping rags., 12. Use both sides of writing paper.

page 52

1. Chad and his friends, look; 2. Chad, finds; 3. He, pulls;
4. rug, takes; 5. friends, come; 6. They, stand; 7. Chad,
explains; 8. rug, seats; 9. Chad and friends, go; 10. They,
fly; 11. Chad, rides; 12. he, hears; 13. She, shares; 14. aunt,
feels, has

page 53

Possible response: Each year, Mrs. Martinez and Mr. Gibson
teach a Greek mythology unit. They ask students to name
their favorite Greek gods and goddesses. Zeus and Athena are
always on the list.

page 54

1. Joanie waited patiently and quietly., adverbs; 2. She had
felt disappointed and rejected before., adjectives; 3. She
really and truly wanted to be a scientist., adverbs; 4. Joanie
read the letter slowly and calmly., adverbs

page 55

1. Patrick studied the wall, and he found a hidden button.,
2. Patrick pushed the button, and the bookcase moved.,
3. Patrick could wait, or he could explore the path., 4. He
wasn't afraid, but he wasn't comfortable, either.

page 56

1. The sunlight shone on the little door., 2. Into the shack
walked Margaret and Danny., 3. A large wooden table was
inside the shack., 4. A black cat lay on the table., 5. Cannot
be changed; inverting would change meaning., 6. Cannot be
changed; inverting would change meaning.

page 57

Corrections of sentences may vary. 1. A box turtle is a
reptile. It lives in woods and fields., 2. simple sentence,
3. It can pull its legs, head, and tail inside its shell and get
"boxed in.", 4. Many kinds of turtles live on land and in the
water., 5. Turtles belong to the same family as lizards,
snakes, alligators, and crocodiles., 6. simple sentence,
7. Painted turtles eat mealworms, earthworms, minnows,
and insects. The musk turtle finds food along the bottoms
of ponds or streams.

page 58

Corrections of sentences may vary. One correction should
consist of two complete sentences, punctuated correctly.
The other correction should be a correctly punctuated
compound sentence.

page 59

1. I was going camping with my friend Michael., 2. We met
Mr. Carl G. Carbur at the camping supply store., 3. Michael
and I decided that we needed a new tent., 4. Mrs. Albright
showed us many different tents., 5. We chose one just like
Dr. Pelky's., 6. Michael's mother, Mrs. Mixx, gave us a ride
to the campsite., 7. After we set up the tent, I walked down
the road., 8. Dr. Pelky was at the next site!, 9. Dr. Pelky
was camping with Mario J. Moreno., 10. Mario showed
Michael and me a great place to fish., 11. I caught some
trout, and Michael caught a bass., 12. Michael and I ate
supper at Dr. Pelky's camp.

page 60

1. My best friends and I plan to tour the United States.,
2. My friend Sandy is very excited because she has never
been to California., 3. She has never tasted any Mexican
food, either., 4. She will be coming from New York and
meeting Jane in Philadelphia., 5. Then, the two of them will
pick up Roxanne in Phoenix, Arizona., 6. When they get to
San Francisco, we will all go out for Chinese food., 7. If we
go to Green's Restaurant for vegetarian food, even Jane will
like the Brussels sprouts.

page 61

1. I found a book of rhymes at the library in Milwaukee., 2. The book was published in London, England., 3. The book contained rhymes from the countries of Kenya, Ecuador, and even New Zealand., 4. My favorite poem told of a crocodile who lived at the corner of Cricket Court and Bee Boulevard., 5. We decided to drive to the Rocky Mountains on Sunday., 6. We finally reached El Paso, Texas, on Tuesday.

page 62

Period placement: 1. end of sentence, 2. end of sentence, 3. end of sentence, 4. after Ms., end of sentence, 5. after Dr., after B., 6. after Dr., 7. after T., R., end of sentence, 8. after J., B., 9. after N., after St., 10. after I., A., B.

page 63

1. My name is C. M. Dooley. I live at 4338 Market Blvd. in Alabaster, Alabama. My birthday is on Oct. 27., 2. Suzy E. Ziegler requests the pleasure of your company at a party in honor of her friend, Maryanne M. Marbles. Please come to the country club at 23 Country Club Dr. at 4:00 P.M. on Tues., Apr. 14., 3. The J. Harold Calabases take great pride in announcing the birth of their twins, Heather H. Calabas and J. Harold Calabas, Jr. This happy event took place on Mon., Aug. 23, at 3:00 A.M., 4. F. A. Jones has been appointed assistant to the president of Bags and Boxes, Inc. This store is located at 45 Ninety-ninth Ave.

page 64

1. Three plants to avoid are poison ivy, poison oak, and poison sumac., 2. Steven, I see that you have some poison oak growing in your yard., 3. "Your dog, cat, or rabbit can pick it up on its fur and rub against you," Wesley said., 4. Yes, it will make your skin burn, itch, and swell., 5. Dana put his clothes in a hamper, and his mother got a rash from touching the clothes., 6. Poison ivy looks like a shrub, a vine, or a small plant., 7. Poison ivy has green leaves in clusters of three, and so does poison oak.

page 65

Comma placement: 1. after interesting, 2. after upstairs, 3. after open, 4. after room, 5. after First, 6. after Next, 7. after while, 8. after addition, 9. after lived, after played, 10. after footsteps, after whispers, 11. after cellar, 12. after Soon

page 66

Comma placement: First letter: after Albuquerque, after April 22, after Dear Ernest, after Your friend,; Second letter: after Albuquerque, after May 3, after Dear David, after Sincerely

page 67

1. ?, 2. !, 3. !, 4. ?, 5. ?, 6. ?, 7. !, 8. !, 9. !, 10. ?, 11. !, 12. ?, 13. !, 14. ?, 15. !, 16. ?, 17. !, 18. !

page 68

Apostrophe placement: 1. Chen's, 2. children's, 3. boys', 4. can't, 5. Won't; Colon placement: 6. 3:30, 7. 6:00, 8. 7:15, 9. Dear Ms. Parker:

page 69

1. You're, 2. you'd, 3. You'll, 4. It's, 5. won't, 6. aren't, 7. mustn't, 8. don't, 9. shouldn't, 10. mustn't

page 70

1. "Have you heard of the Nobel Peace Prize?" asked Emi., 2. "Yes. Mother Teresa and Nelson Mandela have won it," replied Jan., 3. "But do you know who Nobel was?" Emi asked., 4. Jan responded, "No, I guess I don't.", 5. "He invented dynamite," stated Emi., 6. "It seems weird," said Jan, "to name a peace prize for the inventor of dynamite.", 7. "In fact," Emi said, "dynamite was once called Nobel's Safety Blasting Powder.", 8. "Nobel patented the blasting powder in 1867," Emi continued., 9. "He did not want dynamite used for war," he said., 10. He added, "Nobel once said that war is the horror of horrors and the greatest of all crimes.", 11. "How did the Nobel Prizes get started?" asked Jan., 12. Emi said, "In his will, Nobel said that his money should be used to establish prizes in five areas: physics, chemistry, medicine, literature, and peace.", 13. "Sometimes a prize is shared by two or three people," he continued., 14. "I'd like to know more about some of the winners," Jan said., 15. "Jimmy Carter, 39th President of the United States, won the Nobel Peace Prize in 2002," replied Emi.

page 71

1. A Wrinkle in Time, 2. "Camping in the Mountains", 3. "It's Not Easy Being Green", 4. Sounder, 5. The New York Times, 6. Humpty Dumpty, 7. "The Little House", 8. "Why I Like Gymnastics", 9. The Little Prince, 10. "The Owl and the Pussycat", 11. The sixth chapter in that book is called "Animal Language.", 12. A book I really like is If I Were in Charge of the World by Judith Viorst. Items 1, 4, 5, 6, 9, and 12 should be marked with an I.

page 72

1. wisdom teeth, 2. armchair, sunshine, 3. ten-year-old, 4. sky-high, birthplace, 5. slave driver, bloodhounds, 6. storm cellar, smokehouse, 7. hand-to-mouth, run-ins, 8. folk singer, notebook, 9. run-of-the-mill, wallpaper, 10. family tree, best-selling

page 73
1. synonyms, 2. antonyms, 3. antonyms, 4. synonyms, 5. antonyms, 6. synonyms, 7. antonyms, 8. antonyms, 9. antonyms

page 74
1. success, failure; 2. left back, promoted; 3. solution, problem; 4. burning, ice-cold; Answers in chart may vary. end: finish, begin; fast: quick, slow; simple: easy, complicated; gloomy: sad, upbeat; concealed: hidden, open; unsure: undecided, convinced

page 75
Definitions may vary. 1. unearthed, uncovered; 2. nonexistent, does not exist; 3. unable, incapable; 4. discontinued, stopped; 5. improbable, unlikely; 6. inability, failure; 7. resell, 8. insincere, 9. discomfort, 10. mislead, 11. prepay, 12. unorganized or disorganized

page 76
1–16. Sentences will vary. New words: 1. sailor, 2. fearless or fearful, 3. kindness, 4. mighty, 5. happiness, 6. lighten, 7. cloudy, 8. suddenly, 9. quietly, 10. player, playful, 11. wonderful, 12. teacher, 13. magnetism, 14. thermometer, 15. apologize, 16. mythology

page 77
1. air, 2. you, 3. course, 4. would, 5. need, 6. main, 7. mist, 8. can, can; 9. object, object; 10. present, present; 11. spring, spring

page 78
1. week, 2. way, 3. find, 4. know, 5. do, 6. through, 7. see, 8. beat, 9. one; 10–21. Sentences will vary. Suggested homophones: 10. pale, 11. sun, 12. flee, 13. straight, 14. too or to, 15. meat, 16. lead, 17. side, 18. blue, 19. him, 20. pain, 21. horse

page 79
1. to move in a boat; 2. a ship, boat, or aircraft; 3. something a person sets out to do; 4. moved past or went by; 5. gave a name to; 6. arrived at or came to; 7. ended or finished

page 80
Definitions will vary. Suggestions are given. 1. clothing, 2. musical piece made up of parts of other songs, 3. series of questions to gather information, 4. put together, 5. hesitant or unsure, 6. doctor, 7. lie down, 8. enough

page 81
1. to, 2. well, 3. It's, 4. your, 5. Two, there, 6. its, 7. You're, 8. too, 9. good, 10. They're, 11. well, 12. their, 13. it's, 14. two, 15. They're

page 82
1. will, 2. a, 3. are, 4. anything, 5. anybody, 6. ever, 7. any, Sentences may vary. 8. There are no more than four kinds of poisonous snakes in North America., 9. It won't do any good to try to run away from a rattlesnake.

page 83
Sentences will vary. 1. Our family was packing suitcases., 2. Everyone was looking forward to our annual vacation., 3. When all the suitcases were packed, Mom loaded the trunk., 4. We left at noon on Saturday., 5. We drove to the freeway., 6. We stopped often because my little brother was ill., 7. The second day we visited historical places., 8. Everyone enjoyed the rest of the trip, too.

page 84
Senses may vary. 1. blue, sight; 2. cool, touch; 3. large, sight; 4. loud, hearing; 5. chlorine, smell; 6. jagged, touch or sight; 7. rough, touch; 8. soft, touch; 9. warm, touch; 10. delicious, taste

page 85
1. wonderful, 2. Brave, 3. fascinating, 4. hilarious, 5. smile, 6. cheap, 7. soggy, 8. nagged, 9. stubborn, 10. silly, 11. A disaster is more serious than a problem., 12. An antique is worth more than something old.

page 86
Answers may vary. 1. neutral, 2. positive, 3. neutral, 4. negative, 5. neutral, 6. negative, 7. negative, 8. positive, 9. negative, 10. positive, 11–13. Sentences will vary.

page 87
Answers will vary. Possible responses are given. 1. I was very nervous., 2. As I looked out over the audience, my heart felt heavy., 3. I touched the piano keys, and my fingers were stiff., 4. Luckily for me, the performance went very well., 5. As I played the last notes, I knew that I had done well., 6–7. Responses will vary.

page 88
1. as fast as the wind, 2. They were able to whisper, "Hurry! Hurry!", 3. It rode beside him like a good friend., 4. They were enemies that caught at his sleeves., 5–7. Sentences will vary.

Answer Key
Core Skills Language Arts, Grade 5

1. Something that seems unimportant may actually be valuable., 2. It's impossible to change something you were born with., 3. He received a light punishment., 4. She says I give directions from a place where I can't see the road., 5. Don't plan on an outcome until it has actually happened., 6. Doing something in a hurry can lead to mistakes being made., 7. He had a quick and automatic reaction., 8. He tried to blame someone else., 9. It was raining very hard., 10. An exciting life has many varied experiences., 11. I'm undecided., 12. Since something rarely happens, when it finally does, a lot more will happen than expected., 13. She was anxious or afraid.

page 90

Rewritten dialogue may vary, but suggestions are given.

"The boss just called me into his office and told me they wouldn't need my services anymore. He paid me what I was owed, which was only $10. I tried to talk, but he kept writing in a book and didn't seem to hear me…The worst of it, Minty, is that I don't know how we're going to live, or where I'll find work. Times are hard now. I've put us in a hard position."

"Don't talk like that, David May! I don't want to hear it. Get up, wash your hands, and eat your supper; the biscuits are getting cold."

The poor fellow stood up, threw his arms around his wife's waist, and leaned his head on his wife's shoulder…

"Well, maybe we can weather the hard times. I guess I can find work pretty soon, and you'll have enough to eat and wear. I guess we can get by all right."

"I'd laugh if we couldn't."

page 91

Possible responses: Main Idea: how optical illusions occur; Detail: brain compares images you see to images in memory; Detail: brain cannot choose between possible interpretations; Detail: bending of light creates mirages that fool eyes

page 92

1. b, 2. a, 3. b, 4. a; Students should draw a line through these sentences: My mother went to India last year., Cinnamon and ginger come from India., The Ganges is a river in India.

page 93

1. M, 2. D, 3. D, 4. D; Paragraph: Main Idea: Many large factories have been built in southern Brazil., Detail: Some of these manufacturing plants produce cars, trucks, and farm equipment., Detail: Other products of these new factories include shoes, textiles, construction equipment, and leather products., Detail: Many of the goods produced in the factories of southern Brazil are shipped to the United States.

page 94

1. He had a slow and serious nature., 2. He was already an expert rider., 3. The Crow Indians had stolen some Sioux horses., 4. It was considered braver to push an enemy off a horse than to shoot an arrow from far away., 5. Slow had jabbed the Crow with his stick., 6. They had won the battle.

page 96

1. Marc is sad because his friend Thomas is leaving., 2. Marc finds a valuable coin that gives him an adventure and makes him happy., 3. Marc and Mr. Ortiz have dialogue.

page 98

Word choices will vary but should make sense. Narratives will vary.

page 99

Word choices will vary but should make sense. Narratives will vary.

page 100

Answers will vary.

page 101

1. Thanksgiving, 2. Thanksgiving has to be my favorite holiday., 3. delicious aromas of turkey roasting and pumpkin pies baking; lovely autumn colors of orange, gold, red, and brown; sound of children laughing; music being played

page 104

1. pop popcorn in a microwave oven; 2. Two items are listed, special microwave popcorn and a microwave oven.; 3. Remove the plastic overwrap from the bag, and set it in the center of the microwave.; 4. set the microwave to full power.; 5. Set the timer and start the oven.; 6. Shake the bag before opening.

page 107

1. Storing food in cans was developed in England in 1810.; 2. Details may vary. Possible response: A British merchant named Peter Durand came up with the idea. No one invented a can opener until sixty years later.; 3. The can opener that we use today was invented about 1870.; 4. Details may vary. Possible response: It was invented by an American named William W. Lyman. It has only been changed once since it was invented.

page 110

1. The Tasady tribe and the Ik tribe are two examples of people still living in the Stone Age.; **2.** the Tasady and the Ik; **3.** Both are still primitive. Neither tribe knew about the outside world until recently. Both live in mountain areas.; **4.** The Tasady live in caves, but the Ik live in grass huts. The Tasady have plenty of food, but the Ik are always struggling to find food. The Tasady have a good chance of surviving, but the Ik do not.; **5.** contrast

page 113

1. a girl named Katharine goes back in time; **2.** Merlin reversed Katharine's wish in the story.; **3.** Katharine would have won the jousting tournament instead of Sir Launcelot. Sir Launcelot would have been dismissed from the Queen's order of knights. King Arthur's Round Table would have been dissolved and never heard of again.

page 115

Order of reasons will vary.

page 116

1. how Mr. and Mrs. Hak-Tak made doubles of themselves; **2.** It was a very clever thing to do.; **3.** Keeping the doubles was a clever way of protecting themselves.; **4.** Building a house next door for their doubles gave Mr. and Mrs. Hak-Tak extra help around the farm.; **5.** Their doubles became Mr. and Mrs. Hak-Tak's best friends.

page 119

1. Wisconsin should have a "Caddie Woodlawn Day" to celebrate the trust between Caddie and her Indian friends.; **2.** "Caddie Woodlawn Day" would remind people to settle problems by peaceful means. Such a holiday would give people a reason to practice their ancestors' customs.; **3.** The state legislature should vote in favor of this idea.

page 121

1. five, **2.** verb, **3.** noun, **4.** The balloon ... 3, Have you ... 5

page 122

Sentences will vary. **1.** optical, **2.** reflection, **3.** magician, **4.** nature

page 123

1. accident, **2.** despair, **3.** guard, **4.** recognize, **5.** squash, **6.** throughout, **7.** annual, **8.** difficult, **9.** history, **10.** talkative

page 124

1–9. Synonyms will vary. **10–12.** Sentences will vary.

page 125

1. Giants in Myth and Legend, **2.** King Press, Inc., **3.** 1983, United States of America, **4.** 6, **5.** 2, **6.** 51, **7.** 73, **8.** 17

page 126

1. two; hurricanes and tornadoes, **2.** causes of the storms, **3.** when and where the storms strike, **4.** tie it down securely, **5.** They could be broken by flying objects., **6.** when the authorities announce that it's safe

page 127

Zeus's symbols: king's scepter, thunderbolt, oak tree, eagle

page 128

Notes will vary but should focus on main ideas and include abbreviations whenever possible. **1.** Responses will vary but should include a reference to key points or main ideas., **2.** Responses will vary but should include abbreviations for North America and California., **3.** Responses will vary but should include that good notes help the reader to remember key ideas.

page 129

1. c, **2.** e, **3.** a, **4.** d, **5.** b, **6.** f

page 130

Topic and detail sentences will vary but should be related to the chosen outline.

page 131

Answers will vary. Possible responses are given. **1.** Our Old Superstitions, **2.** the superstition of knocking on wood, **3.** the superstition of opening umbrellas indoors, **4.** The custom is 4,000 years old. It began with some Native American tribes of North America. The oak tree was believed to be the home of the sky god.

page 132

Research reports will vary.